Cambridge Elements

Elements in Child Development
edited by
Marc H. Bornstein
Eunice Kennedy Shriver National Institute of Child Health and Human Development, Bethesda
Institute for Fiscal Studies, London
UNICEF, New York City

AUTOBIOGRAPHICAL MEMORY AND NARRATIVE IN CHILDHOOD

Robyn Fivush
Emory University

CAMBRIDGE
UNIVERSITY PRESS

Shaftesbury Road, Cambridge CB2 8EA, United Kingdom

One Liberty Plaza, 20th Floor, New York, NY 10006, USA

477 Williamstown Road, Port Melbourne, VIC 3207, Australia

314–321, 3rd Floor, Plot 3, Splendor Forum, Jasola District Centre,
New Delhi – 110025, India

103 Penang Road, #05–06/07, Visioncrest Commercial, Singapore 238467

Cambridge University Press is part of Cambridge University Press & Assessment,
a department of the University of Cambridge.

We share the University's mission to contribute to society through the pursuit of
education, learning and research at the highest international levels of excellence.

www.cambridge.org
Information on this title: www.cambridge.org/9781009087315

DOI: 10.1017/9781009086325

First published 2022

A catalogue record for this publication is available from the British Library.

ISBN 978-1-009-08731-5 Paperback
ISSN 2632-9948 (online)
ISSN 2632-993X (print)

Autobiographical Memory and Narrative in Childhood

Elements in Child Development

DOI: 10.1017/9781009086325
First published online: July 2022

Robyn Fivush
Emory University
Author for correspondence: Robyn Fivush, psyrf@emory.edu

Abstract: This Element delineates how the narrative expression of autobiographical memory develops through everyday interactions that frame the forms and functions of autobiographical remembering. Narratives are both outward and inward facing, providing the interface between how we perceive the world and how we perceive ourselves. Thus narratives are the pivot point where self and culture meet. To make this argument, the author brings together literature from multiple perspectives, including cognitive, personality, evolutionary, cultural, and developmental psychology. To fully understand autobiographical memory, it must be understood how it functions in the context of lives lived in complex sociocultural contexts.

Keywords: memory, autobiographical memory, narrative, identity, self

ISBNs: 9781009087315 (PB), 9781009086325 (OC)
ISSNs: 2632-9948 (online), 2632-993X (print)

Contents

1 Introduction

Autobiographical memory seems simple to define: memories of our personal past. But this simple definition belies the complexity of autobiographical memory, as illustrated in this narrative from Mandy (this and all names are pseudonyms, and are from Fivush, 2019a, unless otherwise specified), a European-descent middle-class US college student, when asked to describe a significant life experience, the best thing that ever happened to her. I begin with a narrative provided by a young adult to demonstrate the complexity of autobiographical remembering and to highlight the multiple developmental skills and processes that are interwoven in this seemingly simple response (Nelson & Fivush, 2004):

> The summer before my senior year in high school, I enrolled in the summer program for high school students at State University in Minneapolis. I was excited to be in a big city (I am from a small town in Minnesota) and nervous to be away from home. When I arrived in Minneapolis, I was overwhelmed with all the hustle and fast pace of the city life. I spent one month there, taking a course in genetics. While the university enriched my mind, the people I met there changed who I was and helped me discover who I wanted to be. I met many great people there, however there were two girls who I became particularly close with – one was Chelsea, a girl from Minneapolis. She brought me around the city because she was familiar with it. We also lived together in the same suite. I instantly became attached to her within days of knowing her. Chelsea was also in my particular class on genetics so we were also study buddies. She filled the void that was left when I left my comfort zone at home; my family and friends. Then there was Jessica from Iowa. The three of us became best friends over the course of those 4 weeks. We did everything from going downtown to get knock-off designer purses, to shopping almost daily at Steinmart, to getting lost (a lot) on the public transit system. Our friendship taught me so much. I learned how to allow people I barely knew into my life and allow them to know things about me that others do not. Although I only knew Chelsea and Jessica for 4 weeks by the end of the program, I felt as if I had known them longer than some of my close friends. Even now, two years later, we still Facebook each other with updates on our lives and I hope I will be able to see them again.

Memories of our personal past are dynamic re-presentations (hyphen intentional, as described in Section 2.3) of webs of interacting threads that include memories of specific past experiences (e.g., "going downtown to get knock-off purses"), memories of extended experiences (e.g., "I spent one month there taking a course in genetics"), recurring experiences (e.g., "shopping almost daily at Steinmarts"), and autobiographical facts (e.g., "I am from a small town in Minnesota"). Obviously, these memories are referenced to a self – they are *Mandy's* memories, memories of *Mandy's* experiences, and as such integrate the external world with the internal world, to include thoughts, emotions, and evaluations (e.g., "I was excited … and nervous," "I was overwhelmed," "She filled the void," and so on). Furthermore, memories of ourselves are rarely isolated from memories of others, of friends and family (this entire narrative is about relationships with new friends placed in the context of missing friends and family from home). When asked to tell about personally important life experiences, people do not report actions and objects that occurred at a specific point in time; they create richly storied narratives of what happened, to them and others, background information about why this experience was important, ongoing thoughts and emotions that occurred both during the experience and in reflections since, links to other experiences, including the future, and how and what experiences mean for understanding self and others in the world.

Autobiographical memory goes well beyond memories of past experiences, to create a uniquely human story of self, a narrative that defines identity in relation to previous experiences, future plans, families and friends, communities, and strangers, creating coherence through an evolving sense of meaning and purpose in life (Conway et al., 2004; Fivush, 2010b; Fivush & Graci, 2017; Fivush & Waters, 2019; McAdams, 1992). From this perspective, autobiographical memory cannot be studied simply as a subfield within the larger memory literature but actually as a bridging construct that connects cognitive, social, emotional, and cultural development. Autobiographical memory is the glue that integrates our experiences into a cohesive whole through narrative meaning-making.

In this Element, I delineate how autobiographical memory develops in sociocultural contexts through the construction of canonical narrative forms for expressing and evaluating our personal experiences. Autobiographical memories and narratives are not isomorphic (Rubin, 2021), but narratives are the cultural tools used to shape our memories, to differentiate the flow of lived experience into meaningful episodes with beginnings, middles, and ends that link experiences together and link experience to self (Bruner, 1991; Ricouer, 1991). Narratives, as culturally canonical tools for expressing and organizing personal memory, create the interface between culture and the individual. To make this argument, I bring together literatures from multiple perspectives, including cognitive, personality, evolutionary, cultural, and developmental psychology. To fully understand autobiographical memory, we must understand how it functions in the context of lives lived in complex sociocultural interactions. This is an expansive undertaking and requires synthesis across many ideas and domains. Moreover, the dynamic interaction between autobiographical memory and narrative development is a deeply developmental process that occurs over time, both in short periods of time as new experiences are processed and in developmental time across the life span (Fivush et al., 2017).

Thus, the first half of this Element provides a broad integrative theoretical overview, beginning with situating autobiographical memory within conceptualizations of memory and culture and the ways in which narrative integrates the two. This broad-based foundation sets the stage for the second half of this Element, in which I provide a more in-depth review of how autobiographical memory develops within everyday parentally guided reminiscing conversations across the preschool years and how developing elaborative and coherent autobiographical memories links to children's developing memory skills as well as their emerging understanding of self, other, and emotion. I extend this discussion to ongoing developments during adolescence that coalesce autobiographical memories into a coherent life story, essentially a story of "me," which is the hallmark of full autobiography, an autobiographical consciousness that links past, present, and future into an integrated whole that organizes, expresses, and communicates who one is in the world and in relation to others. It is in this sense that autobiographical memory is uniquely human, in providing a form of consciousness that relies on socioculturally mediated tools for constructing a life, and expansive, in integrating memories of self in ways that provide meaning and purpose to a life lived.

2 Conceptualizing Memory

Memory is perhaps one of the most elastic terms in the philosophical and psychological literature. At different points in time over the past 2,000 years, memory has been conceptualized as an archive, essentially an etching in the brain, of everything we have experienced, a repository of all knowledge, equating learning and memory, or as a specific type of knowledge that is defined by self-referential links that separate memory from more abstract conceptual understanding (see De Brigard, 2014 and Sutton, 1998 for reviews). More contemporary psychological attempts to define memory have relied on organizing memory into types or systems. Although there are many nuances, there is relatively widespread agreement that memory can be divided into declarative and nondeclarative systems (Squire, 2004). Roughly speaking, nondeclarative memory is memory of procedures, the "how" rather than the "what." Riding a bike, driving a car, and hitting a tennis ball are all considered procedural knowledge, a knowledge that is not necessarily available to conscious reflection but that guides our actions. Declarative memory, in contrast, is consciously accessible representations of past experiences.

Tulving's (1972) distinction of declarative memory into semantic and episodic has driven most of the research and theorizing about declarative memory. Episodic memory is memory for specific experiences tied to a particular time and a place (e.g., I went to Paris for my twenty-first birthday), and semantic memory is abstracted and devoid of time and place markers (e.g., Paris is the capital of France). Semantic memory can be abstract conceptual knowledge gained through lived experience, or, especially in industrialized cultures that engage in formal education, can be material that was deliberately studied and learned, such as historical and scientific knowledge. The distinction between semantic and episodic memory makes some intuitive sense, but as research and theorizing have suggested, the distinction may not really capture the way memory works (De Brigard, 2014; Dudai & Edelson, 2016). Here, I focus on two issues that have emerged in the theoretical and empirical literature on autobiographical memory, the equation between episodic and autobiographical memory, and the deeper and more difficult issue of the relations between memory systems and memory processes. To foreshadow, and based on the description of autobiographical memory that began this Element, I will argue that autobiographical memory and episodic memory are far from the same and, perhaps more importantly, that autobiographical memory (and perhaps all of memory) is better understood as an ongoing process of remembering rather than as a storehouse of things remembered.

2.1 Episodic and Autobiographical Memory

In Tulving's (1972) initial conceptualization, he defined episodic memory as tied to a specific time and place and as having autonoetic consciousness, that is, the organism is conscious of having experienced a specific event in a specific time and place in the past. Over the years, it has become clear that memories can be tied to a specific time and place without necessarily entailing autonoetic consciousness. This is most evident in the nonhuman animal literature, in which it can be clearly demonstrated that, for example, scrub jays (a kind of bird) are highly sensitive to the specific time and place of food caching (e.g., Clayton et al., 2003), even if they may not be able to "bring to mind" a memory of "self" hiding the food at a time and place. Some researchers have labeled this type of memory "episodic-like" to avoid the criticism that they might be claiming some form of autonoetic consciousness in birds and other nonhuman animals (Crystal, 2010). Human infants are also quite capable of recalling specific events from the past. By the second half of the first year, infants presented with a novel action sequence performed with unusual objects will reconstruct that sequence in behavior even weeks later (Bauer, 2015). What this type of research clearly demonstrates is that episodic memory, memory of specific where and when information, is possible without claiming autonoetic consciousness.

The addition of autonoetic consciousness to episodic memories adds another layer of information for the rememberer – information about *self* over time, the ability to place the self at a particular point in the past, or what is now called "mental time-travel" (Suddendorf et al., 2009). Mental time-travel implies that the individual can "travel" back in time in their memories and consciously bring to mind a past experience. An intriguing added wrinkle to the idea of mental time-travel is that individuals can also travel forward in time, engaging in "future episodic thinking" by imaginatively conceptualizing what will happen at some future point in time based on both specific past experiences and general semantic knowledge about the world (Schacter et al., 2007). Theories of mental time-travel suggest that episodic memory may not be tied to the past but simply be about the "not present." This perspective raises thorny questions about possible differences between memory and imagination (Hassabis & Maguire, 2007) and supports ideas about memory as highly reconstructive, an issue I discuss in more detail later in this Element. The conflation of mentally traveling back and traveling forward in time also raises questions about the separation between episodic and semantic memory – if we use general knowledge infused with episodic thought to propel ourselves mentally into the future, why would we not also be using general, semantic knowledge when we remember the past?

Moreover, bringing the idea of *self* into the theory of episodic memory fundamentally changes how we understand what episodic memory versus autobiographical memory may be. With the addition of autonoetic consciousness, it is no longer simply a specific memory of an event that occurred at a particular time and place; it now becomes an event that happened *to me*. The transition from episodic to autobiographical requires at least three additional layers of processing or knowledge (Fivush, 2010b; Nelson & Fivush, 2020). First, there has to be a reflective *self* that is remembering. Second, there has to be a conceptualization of a *self in the present* remembering a *self in the past*; thus, there must be some ability to construct a timeline. Third, there has to be some way of connecting the *self in the present* to that *self in the past* – that was the same me that experienced that event in the past that is remembering that event in the present – thus the construction of time must be along a personal timeline, a sense of the *me* traveling along a temporal pathway. As William James (1890) suggests, we do not wake up in the morning wondering whose thoughts are in our mind; we know they are our thoughts and that our thoughts are continuous over time. It is this continuity of consciousness that ensures a sense of self that is continuous over time, and this continuity of consciousness requires a continuity of memories, an *autobiographical consciousness* (see also Schectman's theory of a narrative self, 2003).

All three layers of self-understanding – that "I" am remembering, that what I am remembering is something that happened to "me" in the past, and that the past "me" is related to this present experiencing "I" – underlie autobiographical consciousness. Yet, obviously, from a developmental perspective, this is a very complicated conceptual understanding, relying on developments of self-concept, time, and theory of mind (Fivush, 2019a; Nelson & Fivush, 2004; Nelson & Fivush, 2020). More specifically, although there is a nascent sense of bodily self in infancy, toddlers do not recognize themselves in the mirror, a hallmark of self-concept, until eighteen to twenty-two months of age, and it is not until age three or later that toddlers begin to understand self-conscious emotions such as embarrassment that rely on an understanding that there is a self being watched and evaluated (Rochat, 2018). Clever studies by Povinelli (2001) further demonstrate that it is not until age five that children begin to connect the previous self to their current self; children watching a video of themselves in the past do not make a connection between their current self watching the video and the self portrayed on the video, a skill which is fundamental to autonoetic consciousness. Understanding others also develops gradually across the preschool years. The development of theory of mind, the idea that all individuals hold unique thoughts, emotions, and desires, begins with simple empathic responses as early as the first year of life and develops through understanding one's own mind as separate and possibly different from others across the toddler years. It is not until the end of the preschool years that children understand "false belief," that a person can hold a belief about the state of the world that is demonstrably untrue (Wellman, 2018).

Both developing an evaluative self-concept and understanding of theory of mind may be critical developmental skills for a full autobiographical consciousness. To understand a continuous me over time that has specific experiences, I may need to further understand that my autobiographical consciousness is unique, that my continuity of consciousness is mine alone, and that others have their own individual autobiographical consciousness (Fivush & Nelson, 2006). Without this understanding, what I know over time is simply general knowledge of how things happen, similar to scrub jays knowing where food is hidden, and not specific knowledge of what happened to *me* that may be the same or different from what others may know. Thus, we can separate the development of episodic memory for time and place as emerging early in development (e.g., Bauer & Leventon, 2013; Ghetti & Bunge, 2012), and autobiographical consciousness as evolving more gradually across childhood as more nuanced and integrated understandings of self, others, and time develop.

From this perspective, it is clear that both nonhuman and human animals can have episodic memories without autobiographical consciousness and thus not all episodic memories are autobiographical. If we further reflect on the need for a more extended consciousness over time to achieve autobiographical consciousness, a sense of self in the past and the present linked through experience, then it is also clear that autobiographical memory is more than a discrete set of episodic memories. Autobiographical memory weaves episodes into an ongoing tapestry of self, linking earlier experiences to later experiences, linking past experiences to a current sense of who one is, how we became that way, and what our future holds (Conway & Pleydell-Pearce, 2000; Conway et al., 2004), an ability that does not develop until adolescence as I discuss in Section 5.1 in this Element. This is what we see in Mandy's narrative. Her narrative is clearly autobiographical, but it is certainly not an episode. It is an artfully connected series of facts and single, repeated, and recurring experiences that create a sense of who Mandy is and how she became this person, what is important to her, and what she strives for. Research that assumes that recalling a single episode in time and space is the gold standard of autobiographical memory research misses the essential point of autobiographical memory, a question asked by Baddeley (1988, p. 3), "But what the hell is it for?" One answer seems to be that autobiographical memory functions to create a sense of self as continuous over time, essentially a narrative identity.

2.2 Autobiographical Memory and Autobiographical Narratives

Whereas cognitive researchers have focused on memories of past experiences as a problem of understanding the process of encoding, storing, and retrieving specific information, researchers from a tradition of social and personality theory turned to autobiographical memory to answer rather different questions: How do we form a sense a self over time? As just outlined, this question also emerged as more cognitively oriented researchers began to dig deeper into episodic memory as a system. Thus, in the early 1990s, a synergy emerged between the cognitive and personality literatures around this question. In particular, McAdams (1992) outlined a theory of personality that included the life story as a critical layer. Stemming from Erikson's (1968) psychosocial developmental theories, McAdams proposed that individuals create unity and purpose through storying their lives around developmentally critical tasks, such as trust, autonomy, affiliation, identity, generativity, and integrity. More specifically, with development, individuals fashion key narratives that address core developmental issues and express developmental tensions. From these developmentally evolving narratives, individuals construct an overarching life narrative that integrates experiences into a coherent whole that explains how they became the person they are and will be in the future and expresses ongoing consideration and resolution to developmentally critical concerns. The narratives individuals create are based on their remembered experiences, but McAdams did not concern himself with the mechanisms of the memory process as much as the use of memories to create a life narrative that is coherent and explanatory.

At about this same time, Bruner (1990, 1991) reintroduced narratives into the cognitive literature as a basic form of human understanding. Bruner argued that humans are storytellers and that we understand our world and ourselves through stories. Stories are deeply embedded in our ancestral evolutionary history; there is growing evidence that our forebears told stories and likely used these stories to understand virtually all aspects of the world, from its origin to the people in it (Boyd, 2018; Donald, 2001). Stories, or narratives, go beyond recounting actions in sequence; narratives integrate the outer world with the inner world, interweaving what happened with motivations, thoughts, and emotions, bending experience into discrete units defined through beginnings, middles, and ends formed by human intentions and reactions (Bruner, 1990; Labov, 2010). Speculatively, humans came to understand their world through stories – stories of ancestors, great hunters and warriors, chiefs and priestesses – and as these stories came to shape how the world was understood, they became the way we understood individual lives as well. Humans began to shape their experiences into personal stories that explained and motivated human behavior (Fivush, 2019b; McAdams, 2019).

Theoretically, then, narratives are a critical link between cognitive and personality psychology; they are culturally mediated forms for expressing and evaluating experience, both experiences of others and experiences of self. Understood this way, narratives become a key connection between mind and world (Goodman, 1978; McLean & Syed, 2015). Stories that shape our communal culturally mediated understanding of world also shape our understanding of self. Narratives are both outward and inward facing, providing the interface between how we perceive the world and how we perceive ourselves. In narrating our own lives, narratives transform our memories of what happened into stories of what these happenings mean for who we are in the world and who we want to be. Indeed, research on the self-reported functions of autobiographical memory has identified three major functions: to define self, to create and cement social relationships, and to direct future behavior (Bluck et al., 2005). All three functions are both constructed and expressed in autobiographical narratives

(Waters et al., 2014). In other words, as we create stories from our experiences, we form our sense of self, our relationships with others, and project ourselves into the future. This approach fundamentally changes the way we understand what autobiographical memory is for, and how episodic memories are co-opted for it. This is not to argue that autobiographical memories are represented as narratives. Rather, narratives are the way in which multimodal, multisensory memories of our personal experiences are brought together into a coherent, verbalizable, and communicable form (Brockmeier, 2019). If this conceptualization of memory is correct, then it changes our conceptualizations of memory from something we *have* to something we *do*.

2.3 Memory as a Process

Much of the scholarly history of memory assumes, at least implicitly, some form of memory "trace" (Brockmeier, 2015; Sutton, 1998). A memory trace is a hypothetical construct that explains memory as a laying down or encoding of a specific experience in the brain/mind in such a way that the individual can access and retrieve that trace at some point in the future. That is, a memory trace is a reproduction of the original experience that is somehow connected, and even causal, to the current act of memory. This idea has led to research aimed at discovering the way in which memory traces are encoded, stored, and retrieved – issues of capacity, duration, and accuracy – with the underlying assumption that we are encoding, storing, and retrieving some stable *thing*.

Over the years, many of the assumptions underlying the idea of a stable memory trace have been challenged. Both behavioral (Hirst & Echteroff, 2012; Pasupathi, 2001) and neuroscience (Dudai & Edelson, 2016) research have convincingly shown that memories are far from static entities but rather are highly dynamic patterns of activation that undulate over time and with each retrieval (De Brigard, 2014). Rather than a metaphor for retrieving a file from storage, this dynamic conceptualization of memory assumes that some cue, internal or external, starts a cascade of activation that reinstates previous patterns but simultaneously creates new patterns in the very process of reactivation, which leads to a reconsolidation of the pattern in somewhat new ways. Rather than conceptualizing memory as retrieving a trace, memory is conceptualized as dynamic patterns of activation over time. Moreover, even the process of encoding is a dynamic interaction of related previous experiences cued by the current experience. Thus, what an individual remembers is not a representation of something that happened in the past, but a re-presenting of patterns integrating past and present activations. In the words of Faulkner (1951, p. 73) "the past is never dead; it is not even past."

This dynamic view of memory, supported by recent neuroscience research, has, not surprisingly, a long theoretical and empirical history, perhaps best illustrated by the early debates in psychology between Ebbinghaus (2013) and Bartlett (1932). Whereas Ebbinghaus famously sought the memory trace by stripping material to be remembered of all meaning to quantify "pure" memory and map "forgetting," Bartlett argued that it was impossible to strip information of meaning and that humans engaged in ever-present "efforts after meaning" that rendered even nonsense syllables of isolated lists of words to be recalled into meaningful entities. Bartlett's schematic view of memory as dynamic and reconstructive was echoed in the cognitive revolution (Neisser, 2014) and the many schema-based theories of memory that emerged in the aftermath of behaviorism (e.g., Alba & Hasher, 1983; Barclay, 1986; Bransford et al., 1972). Schematic views of memory posit that preexisting information shapes how the individual makes sense of incoming information, and thus reorganizes information as it is encoded in the effort to make meaning. Schema formation begins virtually at birth, with infants initially forming nascent schema from first experiences and quickly generalizing as new experiences occur (Mandler & Canovas, 2014; Nelson, 1986). From this perspective, the function of memory is not necessarily to accurately represent the past but to facilitate understanding of the world in the present and the future (Nelson, 1986; Schacter et al., 2007). By creating schemas that infer and integrate most likely scenarios into patterns of activation, memories are forward facing, providing the best possible information for action in the world.

2.4 Reconstruction, Error, and Accuracy

Over the years, schematic processing views of memory have been integrated with systems approaches in multiple ways, and few theorists actually posit pristine memory traces anymore. But the often-unexamined assumptions underlying the idea of a memory trace still pervade much of the field (see Brockmeier, 2015, for a theoretical and empirical analysis), as can be seen in the idea of "memory errors." A memory error is said to occur when the current information provided by a participant in an experiment does not precisely match the information as previously presented. Schacter (2002) described the seven "sins" of memory as ways in which memory goes astray. The underlying assumption is that memory has somehow failed in these situations. A different interpretation is that memory makes sense of our past experiences in ways that allow us to plan for and predict the future. "Memory" may be best conceptualized as a process of "remembering," a process of constantly reactivating and reconsolidating current and retrieved information to allow the best possible prediction for the present and the future.

Although memory as reconstructive is widely accepted, it is still conceptualized from the framework of accuracy versus error as binary. Research often equates a minor memory confusion with a fully false memory, leading to a view of memory as error-ridden and unreliable (Loftus, 2003). Certainly, in forensic and legal situations, accuracy needs to be defined as an exact match to some past event and as the most important question to be ascertained. Although memory may be adapted for use in situations where accuracy is paramount, such as certain forensic and educational contexts, memory did not evolve within, or to meet, these specific needs. Memory, especially episodic memory of specific people, places, and things, likely evolved to meet ever-more complex social situations in which individuals needed to use information about the past to make decisions about things like whom to trust, where to hunt, and how to prepare for the seasons (see, e.g., Frith & Frith, 2007). In these contexts, where the best place to hunt for berries is where they are usually found rather than where they were specifically found last time, accuracy may be better defined as being able to recall the most likely scenario, essentially the gist of what happened in the past. More dynamic, schematic memory that is dynamically updated and reconsolidated would provide the most accurate prediction for current and future behavior. Indeed, rather than being error-prone, memory is actually quite reliable at recalling the general script or schema, with specific details accurately reconstructed, although confusion and interference among highly similar experiences are likely (Neisser & Hyman, 2000). Even quite early in development, infants and toddlers rely on schema-based inferences (Mandler & Canovas, 2014; Nelson, 1986). Memory "errors" are rarely details that have no relation to experiences in the world; rather, they tend to be highly probable, predictable aspects of experience, and thus are good indicators of what to expect in the future.

This analysis brings us back to narratives as pivotal. By providing coherent meaningful structures that describe and explain human experience, narratives become a core mechanism underlying reconstructive remembering. Whether they are generic scripts or specific stories, narratives provide the frameworks which invite particular kinds of inferences and suppositions that fill in the gaps to create more holistic memory reactivations. Narratives are cultural tools for organizing, remembering, and communicating our memories. But, as I have argued, narratives are not simply individual reconstructions; they are deeply culturally embedded structures that face both inward and outward, creating both mind and world.

3 Narratives as Culture

Narratives emerged as ways of understanding the external world early in our evolutionary history, and over evolutionary time, the narrative forms that organized world-making became internalized as ways of self-making. As such, narratives are a core constituent of culture. These arguments are obviously speculative, but are based on burgeoning archeological and evolutionary research (e.g., Sutton & Hodder, 2019).

3.1 Narratives in Human Evolution

It is obviously hard to pinpoint when humans began to tell stories, but there is converging evidence that multiple evolutionary changes in late *Homo Erectus* were facilitated by and led to the evolution of language and narrative (Boyd, 2018; Donald, 2001). As *Homo Erectus* moved into what has been called the "cognitive niche," the intersection of increasing technology, cooperation and the emergence of language, novel ways of interacting emerged that relied on being able to share what was not present (i.e., communicating what happened in the past). Much has been written about cooperative hunting, which depends on the need for both fine-tuned communication during the hunts and higher quality tool-making, increasing the need to teach tool-making skills among individuals and across the generations (Stout & Chaminade, 2009). Perhaps even more than cooperative hunting, as *Home Erectus* evolved, brains grew larger, infants were born well before full brain development, and needed substantially longer time to mature post-birth, leading to cooperative breeding, with infants and young children cared for in extended groups. Cooperative breeding, in turn, was facilitated by abilities to be especially responsive to others, to trust and empathize with others, and, for infants, to develop socially oriented behaviors to understand and please their caregivers (Burkart et al., 2009). These various evolutions in human behavior that privileged cooperation in hunting and breeding obviously selected for more socially cohesive behaviors, behaviors that relied on more communication and trust. Whereas early communication likely relied on conventionalized gestures (e.g., Donald, 2001), spoken language allowed for a far more specified and unambiguous ability to communicate, thus providing an evolutionary advantage (Dor, 2014).

Again, evolutionary arguments are notoriously difficult and often suspect, but many theorists speculate that spoken language refined and amplified human storytelling (Boyd, 2018; Donald, 2001). Obviously, language developed for and serves multiple communicative purposes, but specifically in terms of storytelling, language disambiguates distant past, recent past, and future times, creates a sequence from simultaneous happenings, explicates the internal world of intentions and motivations, and provides explanations of how one thing leads to another. Through carving lived experience into storied narratives, humans create scenarios of the world, how it *does* work and how it *should* work (Hutto, 2007). Narratives are integral to human communication; about 40 percent of conversational time is telling stories of past experiences (Boyd, 2018); narratives occur about once every 5 minutes in spontaneous family conversations (Bohanek et al., 2009); and we share 90 percent of even mildly emotional experiences with others through stories within 48 hours of their occurrence (Rimé, 2009). Critically, narratives move beyond a simple recounting of what happened to include normative information; to quote Boyd (2018; p.7), "[n]arrative can model and motivate personal values like courage, resilience, resourcefulness, circumspection, and social values like generosity, sensitivity, respect for others whatever their status. It can spread, deepen, and reflect norms." Narratives are adaptive both for within-group bonding and for generational transmission. Telling and sharing the stories of lived experience among group members creates community as individuals begin to understand shared experiences and evaluations, and, in this way, narrative interactions both create and sustain emotional bonds. Narratives further allow for the clear transmission of knowledge, beliefs, and values across the generations. Defined in this way, narratives bear a striking similarity to definitions of culture.

3.2 A Broader Conceptualization of Culture

Culture is a highly contested concept (Jahoda, 2012). Culture has been defined as shared information, in the form of ideas or habits, or internalized belief systems, as a shared language group, as social heredity, and/or a collection of institutional artifacts. Culture has been conceptualized as external artifacts in the world and as internalized world-belief systems. The enormity of even providing an uncontested definition of "culture" indicates the complexity and inclusiveness of this concept. Within psychological science, culture has often been defined in a fairly monolithic fashion, as a group variable in which one cultural group is compared to another (see Rogoff et al., 2018, for a review). Other conceptualizations have underscored intersectionality (Ghavami et al., 2016), with culture being sliced into a Venn diagram of overlapping values, beliefs, and identities held by each individual simultaneously.

I do not intend to provide any complete definition of culture; rather, I will argue that one way to explicate culture is through stories – stories embody culture, and culture is embodied in stories. More directly, narratives may be the pivot point where individuals and culture connect (Fivush & Grysman, 2022; McLean & Syed, 2015). Whether we define culture as internal or external, as behavior or values, as monolithic or intersectional, stories display the complexity of humans acting in the world in ways that both implicitly and explicitly express a shared understanding of that world. As Rogoff et al. (2018) argued, culture can be conceptualized as a way of being in the world, expressed in everyday practices and interactions. And, as already described, stories are a large part of these everyday practices and interactions. The ways in which culture infiltrates and is expressed in stories is, perhaps not surprisingly, best illustrated by a narrative – a story told by Dave, a European-descent middle-class male US middle school student, who told this story when asked about something he knew about his mother when she was growing up:

> Well, she was telling me that they were by the bus stop one day and this kid had been made fun of a lot and that she just didn't want . . . like she was kinda tired of it and so she just said, "Why don't you just stop making fun of this kid . . . ?" and stuff. And it ended up that the bully . . . punched her in the nose. It was just so weird because, first of all, like you don't usually hit a girl. I mean just . . . I don't know; people just say that, but, when you think about it, I don't know . . . But he just . . . he didn't even know her, and he just punched her in the nose, and she actually had to go to the hospital and stuff. And so it just seems like a pretty mean thing to do for the bully and just a really courageous thing to do for my mom, just to stand up for some kid and get her nose broken.

As in all narratives, there are many complicated things going on simultaneously in this rendering. First, it may be somewhat surprising how elaborated and detailed this story is, a story about an event that Dave has not personally experienced, but only knows through his mothers' telling (as confirmed in a follow-up interview). That we tell stories about other people underscores the ways in which narratives allow us to understand the world we have not experienced through the experience of others, one of the defining ways in which language and story advanced human social cognition through the transmission of knowledge across individuals and generations (Frith & Frith, 2007). It also suggests that children and adolescents may know quite a lot about their parents' experiences growing up, an idea I return to later in this Element. Second, the story clearly provides an explicit cultural value system, to stand up to bullies and to be courageous even in the face of possible personal harm. Third, the story expresses some implicit culturally mediated values as well around gender roles. Even as Dave starts to say " . . . you don't usually hit a girl" he begins to hear himself and question this cultural value, "I mean just . . . I don't know." Thus, even in the very process of narrating we are seeing cultural meaning-making evolve and transform, indicating that cultural understanding cannot be conceived as static, but, as is memory, culture is a dynamically emergent process.

In just this one simple narrative, we are already beginning to see how stories work to create shared understanding of the world, of peoples' actions and the values we place on them.

Delineating relationships between culture and narrative expands the ways we both define and study culture. From this perspective, a complete description of any group, however homogenous, is still a culturally mediated analysis (Mistry & Dutta, 2015; Rogoff et al., 2018; Vygotsky, 1978). Cultural research is not only comparisons across cultural groups but further includes an examination of how beliefs and values are embedded within everyday activities within any given group. And stories are a primary means of both transmitting culture and studying culture.

3.3 Master Narratives

One of the critical points of intersection between culture and narratives, and indeed between the individual and culture, is the idea of master narratives (see Fivush, 2010a; Habermas & Bluck, 2000; Hammack, 2011; McLean & Syed, 2015). Master narratives express canonical storied forms of world-making and constrain the forms and functions of individual storytelling in ways that create conformity among members of the same storytelling group (i.e., the culture or subculture). At the same time, master narrative frameworks allow for individual storytelling in ways that dynamically reshape the master narratives themselves over time. Master narratives have been delineated at the level of both the overarching life story, and in terms of specific episodic experiences.

At the level of a life story, cultures provide a canonical biography (Habermas & Bluck, 2000) or life script (Berntsen & Rubin, 2004) that provides a schematic structure to how a typical life unfolds. Life scripts are a form of generalized schema (discussed earlier) that provides the framework for reconstructing what usually happens, whether in one's own life or in someone else's. When research participants are asked to nominate and sequence the most important events that will happen in a typical life, there is relatively high agreement on what events will happen at what developmental point. For example, for most Western European participants, starting school, graduating, finding a romantic partner, getting married, having children, and retiring are points along the typical life script. This may or may not be the life that the participants themselves are living; rather this is the prototypical life that provides the background against which individual lives are lived. Indeed, young children seem to learn this cultural life script even before they have a sense of their own life story (Bohn & Berntsen, 2008); the life script may provide the skeleton on which we each hang our own individual story.

Many elements of the life script seem to be universal, but some elements are culturally specific, both across regionally defined cultures and in subgroups within a given culture, such as gender groups (Ottsen & Bernsten, 2014). Master narratives of the life script do not simply define how a typical life *does* unfold; they define how a life *should* unfold, and therefore provide the implicit cultur- ally mediated normative background that makes sense of individual narratives (Fivush, 2010a). For example, in contemporary US culture, one rarely must narrate how and why one graduates high school, but one usually must have a story to explain why one did not graduate high school. Of course, this example also highlights how master narratives are culturally and historically evolving, both in terms of specific events and the timing of those events. My European immigrant grandfather never had to explain why he did not graduate high school because that was simply not a clearly expected part of the life script in New York's lower east side in the 1910s. Similarly, US women today no longer have to have a story about why they did not have children until their mid-30s – although delaying motherhood is still often stereotypically seen as selfish and risky, it is more common and more accepted than in previous generations (Budds, 2013). (As I return to later, it is still the case that a core master narrative for women in the United States is to become a mother at some point). As these examples illustrate, the life script does bend with sociohistorical change; the cultural life script is prescriptive for individuals, but individual lives begin to sculpt the life script in newly emerging forms, showcasing how narratives are a pivot point between individual and cultural belief systems.

Master narratives also shape how we tell about the specific events of our lives. Some aspects of master narratives emerge from the life script. It would be unusual for someone to say they have no story about the birth of their first child – this is a critical life script event, it is expected, anticipated, and celebrated, and someone who dismisses this event as unimportant would be seen as odd. Note that it is not simply the event that is marked, but the very way it is expected to be told. The birth of a first child is seen as life-changing and joyous, and the master narrative is one of complete bliss on first holding a baby (Kerrick & Henry, 2017). We see this, actually as it is implicitly referenced, in the following narrative by Pamela, a thirty-five-year-old European-descent middle-class US woman narrating a self-defining event:

> The strongest memory I have that I believe defines who I am is the first time my newborn son fell asleep on my chest. This happened about 10–12 years ago but when I think about it the feelings are still strong today and I know this little event is what made me who I am today. I was never particularly interested in being a mother. I was not excited to find out I was pregnant and hated every aspect of the entire pregnancy. I just wasn't sure it was what

I needed in my life at the time. My partner encouraged me constantly and talked positively of all the great experiences we would have but I still wasn't 100% convinced. When my son was born I cried and loved him but it still didn't feel like he was mine. I felt no different, definitely not like a mom how I imagined I would. About 2 weeks after taking him home he was having trouble sleeping in his crib. I got up to get him, propped up some pillows for my back and half lay down with him on my chest. He fell asleep quickly with his hand tightly gripping one of my fingers. I instantly felt overcome with emotion. I felt happiness, calm and peace. I felt clarity, like this is who I am, this is where I'm supposed to be. I knew that my life had meaning.

Again, multiple components of the narrative are compelling. First, as in Mandy's narrative, Pamela places a singular episode, the so-called gold standard of autobiographical research, in an extended temporal framework, from even before her pregnancy to weeks, and now years, later. Second, we see the intricate interweaving of internal and external words – indeed, most of this narrative is about Pamela' internal reflections. Third, these reflections are quite complicated and recursive. Pamela describes how she felt previously, how these feelings evolved, how they did and did not change over time, and ultimately, how they coalesced into this "perfect moment." Note that Pamela does not reconstruct her past to be in line with her current feelings; the story is a story exactly because of this changing internal landscape. So we see memory as dynamic but we also see how autobiographical memory can reflect on both current and past self, as well as the evolving consciousness that connects them over time. In this sense, we can argue that autobiographical memory is meta-reflective in holding multiple reflections about the self in mind simultaneously. Finally, the whole story is told against the culturally assumed master narrative of motherhood – Pamela was not particularly interested in being a mother, did not feel as she "should" have about her pregnancy, and even though she loved her son when he was born, she "felt no different," "not like how I imagined I would" clearly referring to the master narrative of immediate bonding and bliss (Kerrick & Henry, 2017). Yet the narrative ends with Pamela's individual story conforming to the master narrative; she feels calm, peace, clarity, and her life now has meaning.

Much of our individual storytelling about the critical events of our lives is told within the context of master narratives that provide shared meanings and interpretations. Master narratives inform both which events are "tellable" (e.g., the life script events) as well as how to tell them, both in content and structure. Dave's and Pamela's narratives display how the content of their own stories are shaped by culturally mediated master narratives. For Mandy, some of the content may be related to master narratives (e.g., high school summer internship programs, shopping), but her narrative more clearly displays how the structure is formed though master narratives of personal growth. Especially in the United States, there is a culturally shared narrative arc that conforms to a positive self-journey of growth and enlightenment (Perlin & Fivush, 2021). The focus on growth is especially apparent in the "redemptive narrative" discussed by McAdams (2004) as the iconic American master narrative. Redemption narratives are stories of individual grit and determination, of coming from nothing and succeeding, the story that shaped America, of Pilgrims, and immigrants, of rags to riches, still exemplified and glorified in the media today, such as public media stories of Oprah and Dolly. They do not even need last names. They are emblematic of the American story of redemption, although I note in passing that these stories are now about women just as often as they are about men, clearly a change in the American master narrative of gender (Fivush & Grysman, 2022). These stories are everywhere in our shared culture and come to inform how individuals narrate their own personal experiences.

3.4 Cultural Narratives, Media, and Mind

We can discern master narratives expressed in multiple cultural artifacts, such as novels and films, and various qualitative studies have demonstrated the ways in which our own personal stories are influenced by the culturally available stories presented through the media (Breen et al., 2017; Harbus, 2011). Current big data techniques allow us to do this in new ways. For example, Reagan et al. (2016) analyzed The Project Gutenberg dataset of ~50,000 English-language novels using sentiment analyses, which allow parsing of larger segments of text into meaningful units based on similarities and differences in emotions expressed; these analyses convey the shape of the full narrative arc. Nearly all storylines could be categorized into one of six major plots, or narrative arcs that describe the overall shape of the story: "Rags to riches" (i.e., rise); "Tragedy" (i.e., fall); "Man in a hole" (i.e., fall-rise); "Icarus" (i.e., rise-fall); "Cinderella" (i.e., rise-fall-rise); and "Oedipus" (i.e., fall-rise-fall). That a limited number of plot lines emerge from thousands of novels suggests that there may be a limited number of ways meaning is created from experience and that stories provide a somewhat defined set of evaluative frameworks for understanding the world.

How might these culturally mediated narrative arcs shape people's understanding of their own personal experience? Are there similarities between the forms of cultural and personal storytelling? If so, it would suggest that similar narrative forms shape both individual and cultural understandings of the world and of the self. In two separate large data sets, Thorstad, Graci, and Fivush (in prep) analyzed thousands of personal narratives from a heterogeneous sample of individuals living in the United States, aged nineteen to thirty, and found that personal narratives also conformed to these same six major narrative arcs. Analyses examining possible random narrative forms and flat forms (e.g., simple accounts with no narrative tension) indicated no fit. The finding that participants told narrative that express experiences in emotionally coherent sequences suggests that storying experience is a deeply embedded form of meaning-making. Furthermore, that we find the same six narrative arcs identified in fiction in individuals' stories suggests that stories may be the connective tissue between individual and cultural meaning-making. We understand ourselves and the world through a set of culturally canonical story frames.

3.5 The Role of Language

Two critical points emerge from the argument thus far. First, narratives are pivotal: they pivot between being externally and internally facing, integrating actions in the world with thoughts, emotions, evaluations, and interpretations in the mind, and they pivot between the culture and the individual, defining both what shared cultural knowledge is and self within that culture through the construction of a narrative autobiographical consciousness. Second, language is a crucial cultural tool in this process. This is not to argue that consciousness is linguistically formed; it is possible, and even quite likely, that most animals have some form of awareness of their bodies and their surroundings (Damasio, 2012). Rather, the argument is that language allows for a different form of consciousness through structuring of lived experience into narrative forms. Importantly, not all language is narrative (e.g., expositions, description, categorizations, etc.), but narratives build on linguistic form and function (Nelson & Fivush, 2020). Further, there is a specific form of consciousness that is developed through linguistically structured narrative forms that is unique to humans, an autobiographical consciousness, a life story, the story of *me* (Barnes, 1998).

Linguistically structured narrative forms change our consciousness in at least three ways (see also Nelson & Fivush, 2020). First, linguistic narratives construct organized, sequential, and recursive understandings of events. Because language itself is sequential and recursive, in communicating about experiences through language, we create temporally and hierarchically organized sequences of information. But narratives further allow us to move beyond simple sequences to recursively embed sequences into complex hierarchically organized structures. We see this in Pamela's narrative, in which she embeds multiple sequences within the overarching story of pregnancy and birth, with each sequence, the pregnancy, the birth, the aftermath, having its own structure and embedded sequences within the larger sequence. We see this in Mandy's narrative as well, although in somewhat different ways. For Mandy, the organizing structure is "the summer," a temporal chunk such that the only thing that holds the various sequences together is that they occurred during that same time period, with no other temporal structure among the pieces. Yet both narratives create temporal sequences that are hierarchically organized into multiply embedded meaningful units. And both narratives display meta-reflections, integrations of inner and outer experiences. Indeed, for both narratives, it is the internal meta-reflections on the experience that provides the meaning, the connection to self, and, perhaps most important, these inner reflections are themselves recursive, providing information about how these reflections came about and how they changed over time.

Second, language allows us to communicate our experiences with others in fundamentally new ways. Outside of language, we can gesture and point but it is difficult to imagine how we could adequately communicate when in time something happened in the past, let alone anything about our feelings, thoughts, intentions, and motivations regarding that past experience, especially as they may have changed from the past to the present. Furthermore, it is not simply that we can communicate to others but that others can communicate to and with us. We can hear about others' experiences and, in this way, expand our ability to learn about the world, but, perhaps just as important, learn that we may not see the world in quite the same way as others. When we share past experiences together, we share our internal worlds as well, and learn that these internal worlds may be different: we may have had different thoughts and emotions about the event as it was happening, or we may have differentially changing thoughts and emotions about the event over time. These kinds of reminiscing conversations provide access to others' minds that is difficult to imagine outside of language, and help us construct a full theory of mind, the idea that each of us has unique thoughts and emotions that are ours alone (Wellman, 2018). Although, again, it is likely that nonhuman animals have some form of theory of mind (Call & Tomasello, 2008), language seems to play a crucial role in the integrated and extensive theory of mind that human children develop across the preschool years (Astington & Baird, 2005; Watson et al., 2001). Thus language is a tool for constructing a sense of individual minds and human consciousness.

Third, in communicating with others, we reshape our own memories of our experiences. As we share our experiences with others, they offer their thoughts, interpretations, and evaluations of what happened, validating, negating, negotiating our own meaning-making. These reminiscing conversations change what we ourselves subsequently recall about the experience, both the facts of what happened and our own interpretations, in ways that create dynamically evolving re-presentations of the experiences (Hirst & Echteroff, 2012; Pasupathi, 2001). In this way, language becomes one of the ways in which our memories are dynamically evolving over time. Language becomes part of the process of reconstruction. All of these processes are in evidence in this brief excerpt between a middle-class US mother and her four-year-old daughter, Sarah, talking about the previous weekend, when Sarah's friend Melinda had a sleepover:

Mother:	I remember when you were sad. You were sad when Melinda had to leave on Saturday, weren't you?
Sarah:	Uh huh
Mother:	You were very sad. And what happened? Why did you feel sad?
Sarah:	Because Melinda, Melinda say, was having (Unintelligible word)
Mother:	Yes.
Sarah:	And then she stood up on my bed and it was my bedroom. She's not allowed to sleep there.
Mother:	Is that why you were sad?
Sarah:	Yeah. Now it makes me happy. I also, it makes me sad. But Melinda just left.
Mother:	Uh huh
Sarah:	And then I cried.
Mother:	And you cried because . . . .
Sarah:	Melinda left.
Mother:	Because Melinda left? And did that make you sad?
Sarah:	And then I cried (makes "aaahhhh" sounds) like that. I cried and cried and cried and cried.
Mother:	I know. I know. I thought you were sad because Melinda left. I didn't know you were also sad because Melinda slept in your bed.

This is quite a confusing and incoherent conversation. Sarah has some difficulty organizing her thoughts to explain to her mother why she was sad about Melinda's visit. But note that Sarah is already capable, at this young age, of expressing that she experienced multiple emotions, that emotions change over time, and that these emotions are hers. This is already quite an accomplishment. Still, her mother does a lot of work to create some coherence out of Sarah's account. The mother explicitly expresses that there were things she did not understand about Sarah's emotional reactions, reinforcing the idea that our internal lives are our private consciousness, and by the end of this short excerpt the mother has reorganized Sarah's incoherent details into a coherent synopsis of the experience that, although brief, expresses a complicated sequence of multiple causes. As the mother is struggling to make coherent sequential sense of the event – what happened when and why – Sarah is reshaping and organizing her memory with her mother's input. Clearly, this one brief conversation contains only nascent illustrations of these ideas, and no single conversation results in major developmental outcomes. The argument is that these kinds of conversations occur multiple times a day, hundreds of times across the preschool years, in ways that culminate in the gradual development of children's abilities to use language and narrative frameworks to organize their memories with the scaffolded guidance of adults. Through this process, children come to develop an autobiographical consciousness.

From this perspective, language is a mechanism for development. Language is not simply a system for expressing the mind; language shapes the mind (Vygotsky, 1978). Linguistically structured narratives sit at the intersection of external culture and internal mind (Nelson & Fivush, 2020). Language allows for more explicit, organized, and differentiated communications with others, which in turn shapes both the way we are able to communicate with others and the way we understand our own experiences. Again, it is not that language is necessary for thought or for consciousness, but that particular forms of thought and consciousness, such as autobiographical consciousness, are not possible outside of a language-using community. Language shapes and expresses culturally mediated narrative forms, which, in turn, express and shape our individual memories, turning lived experience into the narrative of me. And the creation of narrative is a socioculturally mediated developmental process that occurs gradually across childhood and into adolescence.

4 The Sociocultural Developmental Theory of Autobiographical Memory

If we take seriously the idea that language and narratives sit at the intersection of culture and the individual, that each expresses and shapes both outwardly facing shared understandings of the world and inwardly facing private understanding of the self, then narrative interactions become a critical site for examining development, not just of autobiographical memory, but understanding of self, other, and the world as well. It is in this sense that autobiographical memory is not just a subcomponent of memory, but a broad system that integrates our internal and external experiences into a coherent world-view. Substantial research has confirmed that the ways in which parents and children reminisce about the past influences children's developing autobiographical memories, as well as their sense of self, their theory of mind, and their emotional regulation. Moreover, the internalization of parental reminiscing style occurs gradually, across childhood and adolescence, within everyday reminiscing conversations, and differs both across and within cultural groups.

4.1 Narrative as a Cultural Tool

From the moment of birth, infants are surrounded by stories, nursery rhymes, fairy tales and stories of this family within which the infant was born. Although the specific forms and functions of storytelling may vary across cultures, all cultures studied tell narratives as a core means of expressing experience, meaning, and world-view (Boyd, 2018; Goodman, 1978; Wang, 2021) Well before infants can make sense of these stories, they are being drawn into participating in a storytelling world. As sociocultural theory postulates, skills and practices that will be important for children to develop to become competent members of their culture are omnipresent in the environment, as children are initially onlookers, and as they are drawn into being participants in these activities (Rogoff et al., 2018; Vygotsky, 1978).

One of the best examples for modern industrialized cultures is literacy. Literacy is a critical cultural tool that each child born into these cultures is expected to master to become a competent adult. Again, from birth, infants are surrounded by letters and numbers, on their clothing, their crib mobiles, their toys and blocks, well before they are able to understand what these sounds and symbols mean; they are being sung alphabet songs, and read ABC books, and engaging in counting games. Within the first year or two, children are expected to become at least minimal participants in these games, labeling letters, counting things, and so forth. Expectations for participation continue to evolve, as children are expected to be able to participate in evermore complex ways, as they enter school and beyond.

As is literacy, narratives are also a critical cultural skill. Children are expected to become able to narrate their personal experiences in culturally appropriate ways, expressing what happened to them and what it means. Growing up in industrialized cultures, beginning in the preschool years, children are asked to "tell Mommy what happened at daycare," "Tell Grandpa about our day at the park." When they begin school, children are expected to engage in story sharing, telling what they did over the weekend, over the summer, and such. By middle school, children are asked to write their autobiography. Their personal narratives are critical as they move out into the world, job interviews, college essays, meeting potential friends and romantic partners. Each of us is expected to have a coherent story of who we are, how we became this person, and what our values and beliefs are moving forward, essentially expressing a narrative identity. And narrative identity is forged in early parentally scaffolded reminiscing conversations in which children learn the forms and functions of narrative (Fivush et al., 2019).

Turning to how these processes may differ by culture, developmental research on early family reminiscing initially examined broad differences between cultures that could be generally characterized as endorsing values of independence and autonomy, mostly Western cultures, as compared to cultures that endorse broadly interdependent, communal values, such as Eastern cultures (Wang, 2013, 2016). Theory suggested that within more independently oriented cultures, children would be expected to be able to "own" their experience, telling stories of what happened that include their feelings and emotions in ways that facilitate a more autonomous sense of self. Parents in Western cultures engage in highly elaborative reminiscing that focuses on the child's own internal experiences creating narratives of self focused on autonomy and independence. In contrast, in more interdependently oriented cultures that focus on community and relationships, such as Eastern cultures, early parentally scaffolded reminiscing highlights how the child's actions and behaviors impact the group and show a less elaborative style. Later research developed more nuanced assessments of culture, both in terms of assessing cultures as embracing both independent and interdependent values and of expanding into additional dimensions, such as urbanization (Melzi, 2000; Schröder et al., 2011; Schröder et al., 2013a; Schröder et al., 2013b; Tõugu et al., 2012; Tulviste et al., 2016). Research also expanded to examining within-culture subgroups, such as racial and ethnic communities, and ways in which families with differing cultural experiences reminisced with their young children (Caspe & Melzi, 2008; Cristofaro & Tamis-Lamonde, 2008; Melzi, 2000; Miller et al., 1990; see Wang 2021, for a review). Throughout this research, the guiding assumptions are that the ways in which cultures conceptualize what a life is and how it should be lived, essentially the master narrative or life script, would guide interactions in families that inculcate these values through demonstrating and socializing certain narrative forms that express these cultural values.

Three things must be emphasized. First, research that compares reminiscing across cultural groups takes a broad theoretical perspective on the ways in which self, identity, and narrative are constructed to create, express, and transmit cultural constructions of the world and the people in it. Second, even within this broad-based approach, research has documented individual differences in cultures that allow a more fine-grained exploration and understanding of how the individual and the culture interface to create nuance and difference in cultures as well. Third, the reminiscing literature has demonstrated how cultural values infiltrate everyday behaviors even when studying a homogenous culture. To date, hundreds of studies converge on a robust set of findings linking early family reminiscing style to a host of child development outcomes.

4.2 Early Parent–Child Reminiscing

Parents, and especially mothers, begin reminiscing with their young children virtually as soon as children can talk, somewhere about sixteen to eighteen months of age (Uehara, 2015). At this early age, children are barely able to participate in these conversations; mothers provide most of the structure and content with children providing only one-word responses (sometime nonsense words!) or possible confirmations through head nods or a brief "yes." But even with this limited participation, children are often attentive and engaged in these brief interactions, as we see in this excerpt from a longer conversation between nineteen-month-old Anna and her mother, a European New Zealand family, discussing a visit to a farm (used with permission from Reese, 2013):

Mother:	how many lambs were there?
Anna:	[coughs] do do do.
Mother:	two of the little baby lambs.
Mother:	Gertie and George.
Anna:	heee.
Mother:	and they had little tails, didn't they?
Mother:	what did their tails do?
Anna:	wave.
Anna:	ah.
Mother:	yeah they wiggled and wiggled.
Mother:	and what did (C) give to the lambs?
Anna:	fayah.
Mother:	baby lambs.
Mother:	what did you give to the lambs?
Anna:	is a baa a ah.
Mother:	baby lamb.
Mother:	did you give them a bottle?
Anna:	ayes.
Mother:	you did!

Clearly, Anna is not providing a great deal of comprehensible memory information in this conversation. But she is fully engaged, taking her appropriate conversations turns, providing one piece of information ("wave") and a confirmation ("ayes"), and perhaps some of her other vocalizations indicate some memory. Regardless, what is clear is that Anna's mother takes each of these responses, however minimal, and accepts and validates it, elaborating it into a fuller, sweet little story of Anna feeding the lambs. In these very early reminiscing conversations, we see that children from an early age are being drawn into ways of telling stories about their personal experiences, stories that are narratively coherent and interweave both facts and evaluations – in this story the evaluations that point to appropriate interpretations of the event, that the lambs had little tails that wiggled and wiggled, and that Anna fed the lambs a bottle, indicate that this was an entertaining fun event that they shared and is worth talking about.

Children, themselves, begin to bring up the past as a topic of conversation usually at about twenty to twenty-two months of age (Reese et al., 2019), but at this point these references are most often to the recent past, the berries eaten at breakfast or the swings at the park just yesterday. By 3 to 4 years of age, children are participating to a much fuller extent in these exchanges, often contributing new information and shaping part of the narrative, but mothers still tend to be the guiding force, creating a coherent narrative structure to the bits and pieces that are recalled, as we see in this example between four-year-old Porter and his mother, a European American middle-class US family, reminiscing about the previous weekend's activities with Porter's brother, Alan, and their father:

Mother: Who was keeping you (from going to the museum)?
Porter: Alan.
Mother: Alan kinda overslept on his nap, right?
Porter: Yeah.
Mother: And by the time he got up it was late, so we didn't have time to really get lunch before.
Porter: And I had an accident.
Mother: You had an accident. You're right. And we didn't wanna go to (the museum) if you were having an accident. And do you know what else there was?
Porter: What?
Mother: What'd Daddy really want to do yesterday?
Porter: I don't know.
Mother: What did Daddy do all afternoon?
Porter: Daddy wanted to watch football.
Mother: Daddy really wanted to watch the football game didn't Daddy? (Chuckles) Was it kinda fun watchin' with Daddy?
Porter: Yeah.
Mother: Yeah, but it made us sad that we didn't get to go.

Porter clearly recalls yesterday's activities and adds quite a bit of his own remembered details, including that he had an "accident" that kept the family from going to the museum. Yet, it is still the mother who drives the full narrative, providing the guiding questions, supplying explanations that link actions together, and ultimately providing a complex emotional resolution about both having fun with Daddy but also being sad at not being able to go to the museum. Note that this is similar to Sarah's narrative, with complex emotions being acknowledged and woven into the story, so we are seeing how emotional understanding and complexity of emotional life are already being framed in early mother-guided narratives.

4.3 Maternal Reminiscing Style

In Anna's and Porter's narratives, we see highly elaborative mothers, mothers who are asking open-ended questions, providing narrative content, integrating the child's responses into the ongoing story, and wrapping up the narrative with a concise coherent coda. Since the 1990s, there has been substantial research on ways in which parents, mostly mothers, reminisce with their young children, and how these early reminiscing conversations are related to various child outcomes, including memory and narrative development, self-concept, theory of mind, and emotion regulation. Research has identified substantial robust individual differences in how mothers reminisce with their preschool children both within and across cultures, and has revealed both cultural differences and some striking similarities.

Most striking, both within and across cultures, mothers vary along a dimension of elaboration (see Fivush, 2019a, for a review). Whereas highly elaborative mothers create coherent co-constructed narratives, drawing their children into these conversations, and validating and elaborating on their responses, less elaborative mothers do this substantially less. When their child is not responding, less elaborative mothers tend to simply repeat the same question without adding new information, and once the child responds, the conversation either ends, or switches to a different aspect of the event, rather than building a detailed story. Of note, whereas cultural comparisons indicate that mothers from more independently oriented and urban cultures are more elaborative overall than mothers from more interdependently oriented and rural cultures, within each cultural group, there are individual differences along a dimension of elaboration (Schröder et al., 2011; Schröder et al., 2013a; Schröder et al., 2013b; Tõugu et al., 2012; Tulviste et al., 2016).

Several key aspects of maternal reminiscing style have been established (Fivush, 2019c; Fivush et al., 2006). First, mothers are consistent both across events and time in their reminiscing style. Mothers who are more highly elaborative than their peers in reminiscing about one type of experience are also more elaborative in reminiscing about other types of experiences. Mothers are also consistent across time. Although most mothers become more elaborative as their children develop better language and narrative skills and begin to participate to a greater extent in co-constructing narratives, mothers who are more elaborative than their peers early in their child's development, remain more elaborative than their peers as their children traverse the preschool years, and even into adolescence (Reese, Jack et al., 2010). Second, and critically, more elaborative reminiscers are not simply more talkative overall. Mothers who are highly elaborative during reminiscing are not more talkative with their children in other contexts, such as free play and book reading. Third, mothers are consistent across siblings in their reminiscing style. Mothers who are highly elaborative with their first child are similarly highly elaborative with their younger children. This stability suggests that reminiscing is a unique conversational context, in that it is both differentiated from other conversational contexts and stable within this conversational context. Yet, we still do not know why some mothers are more elaborative than others. There are broad cultural differences, as mentioned above, but explaining within-culture individual differences in maternal elaboration is still to be done.

Many studies have examined child characteristics that might predict more elaborative maternal reminiscing, including gender, temperament, language skills, theory of mind, and attachment status, and the results are complicated. Some aspects of child temperament seem to be related to more elaborative maternal reminiscing in some studies, particularly children's effortful control, a dimension of temperament that assesses emotional reactivity and regulation (Bird et al., 2006; Laible et al., 2013). Children high in effortful control may be better able to engage in extended reminiscing conversations more than children lower in effortful control, but these relations are not found in all studies. Similarly, children's language skills, especially at very young ages, may be related to higher levels of maternal elaboration (Farrant & Reese, 2000), but again, only a few studies have found this and many other studies have found no relations with child language skills. Not only are children's language skills only minimally related to maternal elaborations, it is also the case that children's language skills are only minimally related to their own narrative development (Bauer & Larkina, 2019; Reese et al., 2011). The minimal relations between children's language skills and either maternal elaborations or children's own developing narrative skills underscore that language as a more holistic system (syntax, semantics, pragmatics) may lay the foundation for emerging narrative skills, but language and narrative are not the same.

Some studies reported that mothers were more elaborative with daughters than with sons (see Grysman & Hudson, 2013, for a review), but this result has not been widely replicated and a meta-analysis indicates that child gender is not a significant factor in maternal elaboration (Waters et al., 2019). That same meta-analysis examined relations between maternal reminiscing style and theory of mind and found significant concurrent relations between children's level of understanding mind and maternal elaborative reminiscing, but direction of effect is not clear. It may be that children's theory of mind is a foundation for higher levels of maternal elaborative reminiscing as it provides the basis to reminisce about multiple perspectives. But elaborative reminiscing might also facilitate theory of mind development in helping children understand multiple perspectives through creating narratives such as Porter's and Sarah's mothers did, in which multiple perspectives of multiple people are discussed. One intervention study that helped mothers become more elaborative during reminiscing showed improvements in children's theory of mind understanding, especially for children who began the study at lower language levels, suggesting that children's theory of mind may be an outcome rather than a predictor of maternal reminiscing style (Taumoepeau & Reese, 2013).

The one child characteristic that seems to be consistently related to maternal reminiscing style is attachment. Bretherton (1995) argued that children's early working models of attachment, formed through mother–child behavioral interactions in infancy, set the stage for more elaborated and fluent mother–child communication, and thus a secure attachment may allow for more open and emotionally expressive reminiscing. Note that attachment is a relational variable; although it can be assessed within the individual mother and/or child, the assumption is that mothers and children share an attachment bond, such that mothers who have experienced secure attachment in their own lives would facilitate a secure attachment bond with their child (Verhage et al., 2016). Several studies have shown that both mothers and children who are securely attached engage in more highly elaborative and emotionally expressive reminiscing conversations (Etzion-Carasso & Oppenheim, 2000; Fivush & Vasudeva, 2002; Newcombe & Reese, 2004; Reese, 2008). Furthermore, maternal elaborative reminiscing during the preschool years predicts more secure attachment during middle childhood, indicating that secure attachment may both facilitate more elaborative reminiscing and more elaborative reminiscing may maintain more secure attachment (Oppenheim et al., 2007).

There are at least two reasons why attachment status and reminiscing might be related. First, as the narrative examples above illustrate, mother–child reminiscing is very often about emotional, and sometimes challenging events, and within these conversations, mothers, especially elaborative mothers, often discuss emotions and resolutions. As I will discuss in a later section of this Element, maternal elaborative reminiscing is predictive of children's' emotion understanding and regulation as well as their self-esteem, and emotion regulation is a core part of a secure internal working model. Second, at the most general level, one of the core functions of reminiscing is to build and maintain relationships. Mothers self-report engaging in reminiscing to create emotional connections with their children (Kulkofsky et al., 2009), and more than one-half of reminiscing conversations during the preschool years are about experiences shared with other people, reinforcing the value of relationships (Buckner & Fivush, 2000). By engaging in more elaborative reminiscing, mothers and children are building more intimate and stronger mutual emotional bonds.

Surprisingly, little research has examined other maternal characteristics that might predict an elaborative reminiscing style. Most studies that do examine structural variables, such as educational and marital status, rather than personality or cognitive variables. In one exception, Laible et al. (2013) found few relations between maternal personality variables and reminiscing style. Reese et al. (2019) found that mothers who are depressed are less elaborative during reminiscing than mothers who are not depressed. However, this effect seems to be mediated by maternal sensitivity, with mothers who are depressed showing lower levels of maternal sensitivity during reminiscing than mothers who are not depressed. Relations between maternal sensitivity and maternal elaboration make sense given the relations between secure attachment and maternal elaboration. Related to this line of investigation, there is growing evidence that mothers who maltreat their children show less elaborative reminiscing styles (Lawson et al., 2020), but causes of maternal maltreatment are themselves complex and it is not clear how much the tendency to maltreat is a personality versus a structural inequity variable. In terms of other structural variables, mothers with less than a high school diploma seem to be less elaborative during reminiscing than mothers with at least a high school diploma, but college experience does not seem to add additional prediction (Raikes & Thompson, 2008). One study found that mothers who are rearing children alone also seem to be less elaborative during reminiscing than mothers who are partnered (Artioli et al., 2015). Overall, whereas child characteristics related to maternal reminiscing style have been heavily researched, maternal characteristics simply have not, and much about maternal factors that predict or are related to reminiscing style remains to be discovered.

Although we do not yet fully understand why some mothers may be more elaborative during reminiscing than others, meta-analysis indicates that maternal elaborative reminiscing significantly predicts children's developing autobiographical skills both concurrently and longitudinally (Wu & Jobson, 2019) and maternal reminiscing style uniquely predicts child memory, even when controlling for multiple other variables (Fivush et al., 2006). Maternal reminiscing style seems to be a singular variable that plays a critically important role in the development of autobiographical memory, as well as self-concept, theory of mind, and emotion regulation, regardless of other developmental characteristics or contexts. Before reviewing that research, it is important to emphasize that virtually all the research on reminiscing style examines mothers, often situated within two-parent opposite-gender families. We know very little about the reminiscing environment in different family structures and with different family members, especially fathers.

4.4 Maternal and Paternal Reminiscing

The focus on mothers in the parent–child reminiscing literature must be placed in the context of the wider child development literature, which continues to focus on mothers, more than fathers, as facilitating child outcome (Cabrera et al., 2018). The questions of how and why mothers are assumed to be the more important parent in the developmental literature are beyond the scope of this Element, and would require a more in-depth analysis of the differential roles that mothers and fathers play in the structure, scheduling, and time commitments to family life (see Bornstein, 2013, and Schoppe-Sullivan & Fagan, 2020, for reviews). However, this question itself must be embedded within the culturally mediated narratives of motherhood and the role of women as keepers of family stories. As discussed, master narratives codify cultural expectations and evaluations of lived experience, and motherhood remains a pervasive master narrative.

Although becoming a parent is part of both male and female life scripts, for women it is definitional (Arendell, 2000; Miller, 2005). Women who are not able to have children are pitied and women who choose not to have children are either selfish or, worse, not seen as "real women" and this opinion seems to hold across most cultures studied (Ashburn-Nardo, 2017; Gotlib, 2016). It is not simply the fact of motherhood, but the narrative of how to be a "good mother" that is also pervasive. Cultural narratives of how pregnancy, childbirth, and childrearing unfold in harmony, affection, nurturance, and pure joy permeate cultural media (Kerrick & Henry, 2017). Mothers are culturally assumed to be involved in all aspects of their children's lives and know all the necessary details. Deviations from this master narrative are seen in fairly harsh ways, not just by others but by mothers themselves who feel they are not "living up to" the master narrative (Miller, 2005).

Part of the culturally canonical mother role is keeping the home fires burning, tending the children, making the food, keeping the home clean and comfortable, and keeping track of family members, births, deaths, marriages, and all important family occasions. Women are the "kin-keepers" (Rosenthal, 1985). This role is defined through the master narratives of motherhood and is accomplished through narrative interactions. Women keep the family history and the family stories across tellings and generations. Although this master narrative evolved across historical time and across cultures (McLean & Syed, 2015), it may be rooted in a deeper evolutionary history, as discussed earlier, in which the division of labor necessary to thrive in social groups was initially determined by reproductive work (Fivush & Grysman, 2022). Thus women, more so than men, became focused on relationships and emotional interactions, aspects of experience necessary for providing and sharing caregiving responsibilities. Note that this is not an essentialist argument; if behaviors are adapted to evolutionary niches then they can change, evolve, and adapt to changing cultural niches, and we see evidence in the very gradually evolving cultural norms around mothering, fathering, and child care (e.g., Schoppe-Sullivan & Fagan, 2020).

Currently existing master narratives of gender are seen in at least three ways in individual life stories. First, the master narrative arcs are gendered; for example, Thorne and McLean (2003) found that men told of traumatic experiences using a "John Wayne" master narrative of getting through with determination and grit, whereas women told "Florence Nightingale" stories of empathy and resolving challenging experiences through helping others. Second, in everyday personal storytelling, women and men across cultures differ in ways predicted by the gendered master narratives; women tell personal stories studded with more emotional and evaluative details than do men, and women include more information about other people and relationships in their personal narratives than do men (see Fivush & Grysman, 2022, and Grysman & Hudson, 2013, for reviews). Third, and most pertinent to the focus of this Element, within the family, we see differences in the frequency, forms, and content of parent–child reminiscing between mothers and fathers. A word of caution as I begin to review these findings. This research has been conducted with mostly European American, broadly middle-class Western samples. As yet, we have virtually no data on paternal reminiscing across cultures.

Only a few studies have specifically examined parental differences in reminiscing. Studies with preschoolers, which assess mother–child and father–child reminiscing in dyads, have found that US mothers are more elaborative overall than fathers (Reese & Fivush, 1993; Zaman & Fivush, 2013), but Svane et al., (2021) found no differences between maternal and paternal elaboration in a Scandinavian sample. It is not clear whether this difference is due to historically changing gender ideologies and behaviors, or to Scandinavian values regarding gender equity. Additional research is clearly needed. More elaborative mothers are also more emotionally expressive during reminiscing, and, again, in the few studies that have examined emotional expression during reminisicng with fathers, most find that mothers are more emotionally expressive during reminiscing than are fathers (see Fivush & Zaman, 2014, for a review).

A few studies have also examined families with children reminiscing together, assessing how mothers, fathers, and children co-construct narratives about the shared past. In one study of elicited narratives (Fivush et al., 2009), in which families with a ten- to twelve-year old child were explicitly asked to discuss a time that was highly positive for them as a family and a time that was highly stressful, mothers were more elaborative than fathers when reminiscing about both positive and negative experiences. In another study of narratives that emerged spontaneously during everyday family dinner conversations in families with a ten- to twelve-year-old child (Bohanek et al., 2009), mothers again were more elaborate than fathers in that they provided, confirmed and negated more information than did fathers. A reanalysis of this data set examined the dinnertime narratives in the context of the entire dinnertime conversation (Merrill et al., 2015) and confirmed that narratives account for about one-third of all dinnertime talk, again attesting to the ubiquity of narrative interaction in everyday life. Although there were no differences in maternal and paternal talk about nonnarrative topics (e.g., general knowledge, behavior regulation), when stories emerged in conversation, mothers talked more than did fathers. Although limited, the research is reasonably consistent in finding that mothers are more elaborative and talkative than fathers in narrative contexts.

Yet, there do not seem to be robust differences in how mothers and fathers reminisce with daughters compared to sons. It would seem to make sense, given the theoretical framing of gender differences in reminiscing, that parents would reminisce in more elaborated ways with daughters than sons, yet the findings are inconsistent and two separate meta-analyses have not found child gender effects in either elaboration or emotional expressivity, at least for maternal reminiscing (Aznar & Tenenbaum, 2020; Waters et al., 2019). To complicate understanding of gender differences in reminiscing, by the end of the preschool years, girls are narrating their personal past in more elaborated, detailed, and emotionally expressive ways than are boys and continue to do so throughout childhood and adulthood (Grysman & Hudson, 2013). And in the study of dinnertime conversations just described, Merrill et al. (2015) found that ten- to twelve-year old girls contributed more to the co-constructed family narrative than did ten- to twelve-year-old boys, even within the same family, mirroring the finding with mothers and fathers. Furthermore, daughters of mothers who were more elaborative in the narrative context were themselves more elaborative than their peers with less elaborative mothers. So it seems that girls participate in a more elaborative narrative style, but a more elaborative reminiscing style does not seem to be directly socialized in parent–child reminiscing conversations. This truly is a paradox, and deserves further research attention, especially considering the far-reaching impact of elaborative reminiscing on multiple developmental outcomes.

4.5 How Maternal Reminiscing Matters

Thus far, the research has established robust individual differences in maternal reminiscing along a dimension of elaboration, both within and across cultures. Within a theoretical framework that posits that autobiographical memories are expressed and communicated through culturally mediated narrative forms that provide schema for understanding and evaluating personal experience and the formation of an autobiographical consciousness, we would predict that maternal reminiscing style would be a critical mechanism for facilitating children's developmental outcome in multiple domains, especially: (1) for children's own developing autobiographical narratives, as well as their memories, given that narratives are a cultural tool for organizing memory and (2) for children's developing concepts of self and other as narratives of personal experience integrate external actions with internal thoughts and emotions in ways that highlight the workings of minds. This section reviews the research on these developing relations during the preschool years, as children are enculturated into the forms and functions of reminiscing. The following section extends these arguments into the adolescent years, when the formation of a narrative identity becomes a critical developmental task (Habermas & Bluck, 2000).

4.5.1 Memory and Narrative

The complex interrelations between autobiographical memory and narratives were discussed earlier in this Element; elaborative maternal reminiscing is related to outcomes in both domains. Perhaps the most direct theoretical link between elaborative maternal reminiscing and child outcomes is to children's own developing autobiographical narratives. Indeed, Wu and Jobson (2019) and Waters et al. (2019) showed in meta-analyses of dozens of studies that higher levels of maternal elaborative reminiscing are related to more coherent and more detailed children's autobiographical narratives both concurrently and over time. In the most enduring longitudinal study of maternal reminiscing, Reese and colleagues (Reese, Jack et al., 2010; Reese, Yan et al., 2010) have followed families beginning when the children were eighteen months of age into adolescence and early adulthood. Adolescents whose mothers had been highly elaborative when they were preschoolers subsequently had an earlier age of first memory and a more coherently organized life story, suggesting that the early reminiscing environment laid a foundation for the development of an elaborated coherent personal life narrative.

This research, although longitudinal, is still correlational. Several studies have explicitly trained mothers to be more elaborative during reminiscing, by asking more open-ended questions, by following in and integrating their children's responses into the ongoing narrative, and by confirming and validating their children's participation. Mothers easily adopt a more elaborative style and continue to reminisce in more elaborative ways over a period of weeks and years, compared to mothers who did not undergo training. More to the point, children of mothers who were trained to be more elaborative narrated their own past in more coherent and detailed ways than did children of mothers who did not undergo training (Boland et al., 2003; Peterson et al., 1999; Reese & Newcombe, 2007; Reese et al., 2020), indicating a causal relation between maternal elaborative reminiscing and children's developing detailed and coherent autobiographical narrative skills.

Relations also emerged between elaborative maternal reminiscing and children's memory conceptualized more broadly. These relations have been demonstrated in two ways. First, more elaborative reminiscing about a specific experience facilitates children's abilities to recall details of that experience, both verbally and nonverbally. In a series of studies conducted in the home, Haden et al. (2001) asked mothers and their preschoolers to engage in a planned series of events and video recorded the spontaneous interaction. They then asked children to recall those events. Children best recalled those aspects of the experience that the mother and child both elaborated on during play. Things the child noticed, and even commented on, but that the mother did not elaborate on were poorly recalled, indicating that maternal elaboration helps children encode experience more deeply.

More direct experimental evidence comes from a series of studies by Salmon and colleagues (Conroy & Salmon, 2006; McGuigan & Salmon, 2004). They asked four-year-old children to engage in structured novel play events in the laboratory under three conditions: an elaborated discussion before the event occurred explaining what would happen (anticipatory elaboration), an elaborated conversation during the event itself (elaborative encoding), and an elaborated reminiscing about the event after it occurred. Children's memories of the experience were assessed several weeks later both in verbal recall and behavioral reenactment of the event. Both verbal and behavioral recall were enhanced for the elaborated reminiscing condition as compared to elaborated anticipation; elaborated encoding enhanced recall over anticipation but not to the extent that elaborated reminiscing did. These studies suggest that elaborated reminiscing may facilitate consolidation and subsequent strength and cohesion in remembering specific experiences. In the framework presented earlier in the Element, elaborated reminiscing provides opportunities for young children to practice the skills of re-presenting experiences to mind, and through sharing them with others, to create more coherent and cohesive patterns of activation that allow for subsequent remembering.

Elaborative reminiscing may further help children learn skills for more deliberate forms of memory. Deliberate memory, the ability to intentionally commit information to mind in a declarative sematic form, is an important skill in literate cultures in which formal education is valued (Mistry & Dutta, 2015). Elaborative maternal reminiscing may help children better understand and practice intentional processes involved in deliberate memory tasks through the use of open-ended questioning and reflective back-and-forth co-construction of a coherent narrative. Preschool children of more highly elaborative mothers during a reminiscing task subsequently display better memory in an object sorting and recall task two and three years later (Rudek, 2004). Langley et al. (2017) found similar results, but only at school entry; by age 6, there were few differences in performance on this task between children of more or less elaborative mothers, suggesting that maternal elaborative reminiscing style may jumpstart skills in deliberate remembering, but it is not the only important factor. Experiences in the classroom are critical as well: Teachers also display individual differences in elaborative style that are related to child outcomes, and children's educational outcomes may benefit from exposures to both an elaborative maternal reminiscing style and an elaborative teaching style (Andrews & Van Bergen, 2020).

4.5.2 Understanding Self and Other

As highlighted throughout this Element, autobiographical memory is a broad integrative system that bridges memories of our past with our sense of self, other, and the world in the present and into the future, creating an autobiographical consciousness. As such, children's developing autobiographical memory skills are closely linked to their developing understanding of self and other, what has been labeled "theory of mind" in the developmental literature (Wellman, 2018). Although there is controversy over whether theory of mind actually constitutes a "theory" that children have about self and other, there is little doubt that human children develop the understanding that they have minds, internal thoughts, emotions, beliefs and desires that both persist and change over time. Others also have minds with these characteristics, and one's own and others' minds may be the same and/or different, sharing an emotion, interpretation, evaluation, or seeing things in a different light. Although many other animals have been shown to have some form of this kind of understanding, only human children develop this complex, meta-reflective understanding of mind of self and other that allows for iterative reflection (Call & Tomasello, 2008). Given that autobiographical reminiscing is about experiences of self and other, it is not surprising to find close connections between these developing skills, although it is important to underscore that both self-concept and theory of mind are themselves extremely complicated developmental constructs that are multiply determined; maternal reminiscing style is part of this complicated picture (see Nelson & Fivush, 2004 for a full developmental model).

Specifically, elaborative maternal reminiscing is related to the complexity of children's self-concept. As highly elaborative mothers highlight the links between the internal and external worlds, as we saw in the narrative examples earlier, children begin to develop a more differentiated sense of self, a self that is understood both to have certain traits and to value certain traits, as illustrated in this narrative between four-year-old Jennifer and her mother, discussing the previous weekend when Jennifer misbehaved by yelling at her mother:

Mother:	... You- you had to go to your bedroom, right? Because you didn't ... you were not behaving ... Oh, I think because, something, I asked you something, and you scream a- you scream at me. Right? You yell at me. And that's wrong, right? You can't do that. That's not the right way. You need to talk-
Jennifer:	Sorry Mommy.
Mother:	Oh, it's ok, baby, I told you that, that it was ok. You just need to learn ... Hm? Alright. So are you gonna do- are you gonna, are you gonna scream at Mommy again?
Jennifer:	Mm-mm.
Mother:	No? You're gonna talk in a, in a good way, right?
Jennifer:	Mhm.
Mother:	Very softly, and with a, with a nice tone of voice ... huh?
Jennifer:	(unintelligible)
Mother:	You are always nice, sweetie, (kisses child). Love you. Alright.

Jennifer's mother begins with an admonishment, explaining consequences of Jennifer's bad behavior, but once Jennifer apologizes, her mother quickly pivots to forgiveness, and places the previous bad behavior in a larger context of how sweet Jennifer is as a person. In this way, Jennifer's traits are privileged as more informative than the specific behavior and the admonishment is to behave in future according to these traits. Here Jennifer's behavior is placed in the context of demonstrating who she is *not*, rather than who she is, indicating the complexity of the developmental task of constructing a differentiated, yet consistent sense of self. Notice also that the relationship is restored as loving to end this conversation, echoing the earlier discussion about reminiscing as building and maintaining secure attachment relationships.

Children of mothers who reminisce in highly elaborative ways understand their own traits with more clarity and differentiation (I am like this and not so much like that) than children of less elaborative mothers (Bird & Reese, 2006; Fivush, 2007). Furthermore, this relation seems to hold across cultures (see Wang, 2016, for a review) and possibly across subcultural groups in the United States (Miller, et al., 1990). Importantly, however, the values placed on various self-concepts and traits vary by culture, along the lines of autonomy, independence, assertiveness, and communion. Thus, what is culturally universal is the role of maternal elaborative scaffolding in drawing children into culturally appropriate understanding of their selves engaging in the world, but what is culturally variable is the emphasis on, and self-evaluations of, certain traits over others. Self is at least partially constructed in maternally scaffolded reminiscing that interprets and evaluates children's experiences and behaviors in the context of culturally mediated conceptions of personhood.

Jennifer's narrative is specifically focused on Jennifer's traits and behaviors and how they should be integrated within the larger context of who Jennifer is as a person. In Sarah's and Porter's narratives above, we also see how the child's individual perspective is discussed alongside others' perspectives which might be different from the child's own. The ability to integrate multiple perspectives, both how one's own perspective changes over time, and how one's own perspective may be the same or different from others' perspectives, is a critical building block for understanding that one has unique access to one's own experiences. This integration is a core component of a developing autobiographical consciousness. More elaborative maternal reminiscing is related to higher levels of understanding theory of mind (see meta-analysis by Waters et al., 2019), but the direction of effect may be complicated to unpack. Most likely, higher levels of theory of mind development allow for more complex reminiscing and more complex reminiscing expands understanding of mind (see Fivush & Nelson, 2006, for extended discussion). Critically, however, understanding one's own perspective as unique emerges largely through social interaction that positions multiple perspectives within the same narrative rendering of an experience, and as discussed earlier in this Element, language is a crucial tool in this process. Understanding that I see the world through my own unique perspective through time is forged in social interactions that highlight and define internal worlds.

Of course, in discussing perspectives of self and other, and interpreting and evaluating experience, mothers and children reminisce specifically about emotions – what emotions are, how we experience and express them (perhaps inappropriately as Jennifer's narrative illustrates), and how we resolve them, especially if they are negative. For example, here is four-year-old Zoe and her mother reminiscing about Zoe being scared during a thunder storm:

Mother:	And what happens when there's a big thunder and lightning storm?
Zoe:	I'd want to be with my mom and dad (whispering)
Mother:	Yes, you want to be with your mom and dad. And what happens if you're sleeping and there's a big bunch of thunder in the middle of the night? What happens sometimes?
Zoe:	Scared
Mother:	Scared. Do you tremble like that? Do you shake? Huh? Then what do you do?
Zoe:	I get up and go to my mom and dad (whispering).
Mother:	You get up and go to your mom and dad. And what do we do?
Zoe:	Say don't worry
Mother:	Say don't worry. Do we hold you?
	(Zoe nods yes)
Mother:	Yes, does holding help when you're scared?
	(Zoe nods yes)
Mother:	Yes.

First, notice that this is a recurring event rather than a specific episode, underscoring how autobiographical memory is a medley of types of events, as discussed earlier. Second, Zoe is quite articulate, providing rather long and complex answers to her mothers' questions. Even so, it is still the mother who moves the reminiscing conversation forward; once Zoe volunteers the emotion word, that she is scared, her mother elaborates on the bodily sensations of being scared, but then immediately moves to regulation – what Zoe can do to make herself feel better – and the narrative ends with a clear reassurance that Zoe will be safe (again we see secure attachment themes emerging). Mothers who are more elaborative during reminiscing are also more emotionally expressive, and more elaborative mothers have children who have higher levels of emotion understanding and regulation both concurrently and longitudinally (Laible et al., 2013; Salmon & Reese, 2016). As children learn to understand the causes and consequences of their own emotional experience through coherent narratives, they become better able to use these coherent regulated narratives of the past to cope in the present.

Constructions of emotion vary by culture (De Leersnyder et al., 2015). Very broadly conceptualized, more independently oriented autonomous cultures value individual emotional experience whereas interdependently oriented communal cultures downplay emotions that create divisions, such as anger, and emphasize emotions that create community, such as shame. Mothers in more independently oriented autonomous cultures include more emotions overall when reminiscing than do mothers in interdependently oriented communal cultures, and they focus more on emotions experienced by the children themselves rather than emotions of other people (see Wang, 2013, 2021, for reviews). Mothers in more interdependently oriented cultures reminisce about emotions within didactic contexts that focus on how the child's behaviors affect others (Fivush & Wang, 2005). Still, regardless of cultural orientation, the linkages between maternal reminiscing and emotional understanding are similar across cultures. More elaborative emotionally expressive mothers within each culture have children who display higher levels of emotion understanding and regulation concurrently and over time. Again, we see cultural variation in focus of narrative reminiscing in ways that conform to canonical cultural values, yet similar processes in the ways on which maternal reminiscing are linked to child outcome.

Clearly, the developing interconnections between reminiscing, memory, and understanding of self, other, and emotion are dynamic and dialectical. Across hundreds of reminiscing conversations across the preschool years, mothers and children are co-constructing narratives that incorporate multiple perspectives on their experiences, the thoughts and emotions of different people, and how their own thoughts and emotions change over time. Emerging conceptions of self, other, and emotion feedback into these reminiscing conversations in ever-spiraling ways, creating a mosaic of dynamic autobiographical memories, memories of self and other emotionally intertwined through socially constructed narratives embedded in cultural contexts. As children transition into middle childhood, they are narrating fairly coherent and complex autobiographical narratives about themselves and others, as this example of seven-year-old Megan, a European-descent US school child narrates when asked by an unfamiliar female adult interviewer about a time that Megan felt lonely or left out:

> Well, I have a best friend at school and her name is Christina, and she has a nice friend that I like a lot. She was just coming over for like two or three months. Her name is Camille and she is from France. And one time I felt really left out because she was only going up to Camille and not me. [Interviewer: Oh really?] I felt left out. [Interviewer: What else about that?] Um, but then we tried to get her to talk to me . . . and I got to play with them.

Clearly, Megan is providing a coherent and emotionally compelling narrative about her lived experience. She begins by orienting her listener to the setting and characters before moving into the specific events that were problematic for her. Although she needs a bit of nondirective prompting from the interviewer to complete the narrative, she ends with a strategy to solve the problem and a resolution. Although brief, it is well-formed narrative that places Megan and her friends in a larger life context, describes relations between self and others, and integrates internal thoughts and feelings with external events. But this is not yet an autobiography. It is not until adolescence that children achieve a full sense of autobiographical consciousness, a narrative identity that is continuous through time.

5 Adolescence, the Life Story, and the Intergenerational Self

One of the critical functions of autobiographical memory laid out at the beginning of this Element is to create a sense of coherence and consistency of self over time (Conway, et al., 2004). Autobiographical memory moves beyond memories of single discrete episodes to weave experiences into a continuous life story, how single episodes, recurring events, and extended events are braided together to define the person we are, how we became this way, and what we will become, integrating past, present, and future into a continuous *me*, a narrative identity (McAdams, 1992). Through culturally mediated reminiscing interactions across the preschool years, children come to develop reasonably coherent narratives of discrete episodes that begin to define their developing understanding of self and other, creating the foundation for an autobiographical consciousness. But as yet, these discrete episodes are not linked to each other in globally causal ways or to a continuous identity over time. When asked to tell the story of their lives, children in middle childhood, between the ages of six and eleven or so, will provide a few discrete episodes ("Last year my birthday party was at Chucky Cheese"; "The other day I hit a home run"), perhaps a recurring event or two ("I play baseball every Sunday with my brother") along with mentioning enduring characteristics and evaluations ("I love playing baseball. I am a really good batter") (Bohn & Bernsten, 2008; Habermas & Köber, 2014). As children develop into adolescence, they begin to bring these various discrete autobiographical memories into an overarching timeline in which personally subjective experiences are both temporally and causally connected, creating a full autobiographical consciousness.

5.1 Time, Perspective, and Autobiographical Reasoning

Two key cognitive advances develop across middle childhood and adolescence that undergird autobiographical consciousness, both based on advances in abstract thinking: perspective-taking skills and understanding of time. Earlier theory of mind understanding sets the stage in adolescence for more abstract hypothetical forms of perspective taking that allows adolescents to iteratively think about their own and others' minds – thinking about what one is thinking, thinking that others are thinking about what they are thinking, thinking about others thinking about you, and so forth, with a meta-perspective, or third-person perspective that oversees all of these perspectives, either integrating them or being able to hold multiple, perhaps even conflicting, perspectives in mind simultaneously (Hall et al., 2021). This kind of abstract meta-reflective thinking about mind of self and other allows adolescents to begin to think in more hypothetical and reflective ways about how experiences shape understanding of self and, at the same time, how reflections on self can shape the way we think about our experiences, leading to a kind of meta-narrative of self and other.

A second cognitive advance is understanding of time (see Friedman, 2003, for a full review). Although preschoolers have a rudimentary conception of "today," "tomorrow," and "yesterday," they have difficulty actually differentiating when in the past specific events occurred. Preschoolers can judge recency between events if they were in the recent past but have difficulty for events in the remote past. Through middle childhood, children continue to have difficulty ordering sequences of events in time (e.g., Canada et al., 2020), and they have difficulty sequencing annually occurring events in relation to each other (was Christmas before or after your birthday?). Children can use seasonal and time of day information (it was winter; it was morning) to judge when events occurred, but it is not until early adolescence that children are using conventional clock and calendar time consistently to order events, placing the events of their life along a timeline marked by conventional years, months and dates. The ability to order one's own experiences on a personal timeline is a gradual process across middle childhood, culminating in adolescence and allowing for the construction of a coherent temporally ordered life story (Habermas & Köber, 2014; Köber & Habermas, 2017).

As adolescents begin to order their life experiences along a personal timeline, and reflect on multiple perspectives on their experiences, they also begin to make more explicit connections between self and events (Pasupathi et al., 2007) and engage in autobiographical reasoning that provides causal linkages between the experiences one has had and the person one has been and will become (Habermas, 2011). We see this in Mandy's narrative at the beginning of the Element. Mandy quite explicitly narrates how the summer experiences were shaped by her biographical experiences (being overwhelmed because she is from a small town) but also shapes her emerging perspective on who she is (the people I met there changed who I was; I learned how to allow people I barely knew into my life) and who she wants to be in the future (the people I met there . . . helped me discover who I wanted to be). In constructing this experience, Mandy places it at a particular point in her own autobiographical life story (the summer before my senior year; two years ago), and explains who she was as she entered into this experience and who she became as a result of it. This kind of temporal- and self-perspective turns memories into autobiography (Fivush et al., 2011). Furthermore, just as in the preschool years, these developmental milestones are achieved through participating in local everyday reminiscing conversations.

5.2 Maternal Scaffolding of Life Stories

Habermas and colleagues (Habermas & de Silveria, 2008; Habermas et al., 2010; Habermas & Paha, 2001) have conducted longitudinal studies examining the development of life stories as well as how they emerge within maternally scaffolded reminiscing conversations. When children first begin to construct their autobiographical memories along a timeline, at about ten years old, they rely on chronological order; by mid-adolescence, they begin to engage in autobiographical reasoning, creating links between chronologically ordered events that connect biographical facts and personal characteristics that create personal coherence to their life stories. By the end of the adolescent years and early adulthood, adolescents are constructing hierarchically embedded episodes within episodes, with both within and across episode links that tie events together into larger and larger meaningful units, (when I went to science camp; my first year of high school), creating more extended life periods (elementary school, high school), and tie events and units to self (because I went to science camp, I became really interested in astronomy and so in high school I pursued honors science and will study astronomy in college).

Eventually autobiographical memory becomes organized hierarchically as life periods defined both temporally (school, first job) and thematically (romantic relationships, work life), with specific episodes, recurring experiences, and extended events arrayed along multiple intersecting timelines, and dynamically accessible depending on current self needs and goals (Conway & Pleydell-Pearce, 2000). The early reminiscing environment continues to influence autobiographical memory and narrative development into the adolescent years. Reese and colleagues (Reese, Jack et al., 2010; Reese, Yan et al., 2010) followed families from when the child was eighteen months of age into adolescence. Adolescents whose mothers were more elaborative during the preschool years provided an earlier age of first memory, a more coherent and differentiated life story in the form of more complicated subepisodes, and also showed higher self-esteem.

But obviously, reminiscing does not end with the preschool years. Families continue to reminisce about the past, and these everyday reminiscing conversations continue to be impactful. Parental (again mostly maternal) scaffolding of life stories continues to play a major role in adolescents' developing life story, with mothers providing structure just beyond what adolescents can produce on their own (Habermas & de Silveria, 2008; Habermas et al., 2010; Habermas & Paha, 2001). Early in the process, at about ten to twelve years of age, mothers focus on helping children place their life experiences on a chronological time-line. Once children master these skills, mothers extend their scaffolding to include self-event connections and biographical links, which children then begin to incorporate into their own stories. Finally, in late adolescence, mothers scaffold fully evaluative life stories with hierarchically organized temporal and evaluative coherence, and these same abilities emerge in adolescents themselves. Although there is still limited research on maternal scaffolding of life stories, these studies have provided invaluable information about how life stories are scaffolded in everyday reminiscing conversations which model autobiographical reasoning in more chronologically and causally coherent ways. By the end of adolescence, we see autobiographical narratives like Mandy's, replete with iterative single and recurring episodes and explicit interpretation and evaluation of life experiences.

5.3 Social and Cultural Contexts of Life Stories

Everyday reminiscing conversations are embedded within larger sociocultural worlds that provide canonical narratives that define, explain, and evaluate lives. As children grow into adolescence, and develop more abstract temporal and perspective-taking skills, the social and cultural worlds around them also begin to expand and expect them to transition into culturally competent adults, making decisions about who they want to be, what they want to do, and what they are committed to, in multiple domains, including professional, personal, religious, and political. Essentially adolescents enter into what Erikson (1968) called a "crisis of identity." With new skills and new sociocultural demands placed on them, adolescents begin a process of exploration that, hopefully, culminates in a healthy achieved adult identity. This identity is constructed within the culturally available narrative frameworks for defining a life. In addition to reminiscing conversations that help shape adolescents' own personal experiences into canonical narrative forms, adolescents also begin to seek out and use a wider set of cultural narratives to model their own life story, and this happens both within the family and in the wider cultural context.

5.3.1 Family Reminiscing and the Intergenerational Self

Not surprisingly, as children develop into adolescents, family reminiscing conversations become more complex and multifaceted. Whereas the vast majority of parent-preschool reminiscing conversations focus on the child's own lived experiences, helping children express personal experience in culturally appropriate ways, as children develop into adolescents, stories of self become more embedded in stories of others. To explore the everyday context of family reminiscing with preadolescents, Fivush and colleagues recorded dozens of broadly middle-class US families with ten- to twelve-year old children conversing around the dinner table (Bohanek et al., 2009; Fivush & Merrill, 2016; Merrill et al., 2015). Dinner conversations ranged from behavioral regulation (sit down, please pass the salt) to general knowledge (a new theater being built in town, how electricity works), with about one-third of the entire conversation being family narratives. A narrative emerged about every 5 minutes, and these narratives were both extended and highly participatory, confirming that narrative interactions are a frequent and sizable part of everyday conversation. About one-half of all narratives were "Today I . . . " narratives, stories about what happened to the narrator that day, catching the family up on daily trials and tribulations, achievements and interactions. Of note, whereas about one-half of the "Today I . . . " stories were about the child, about one-half were about the parent's day at work. That parents tell many stories about their daily experiences demonstrates that children are being exposed to unknown worlds through stories; that these stories are about parents, individuals who are critical identity figures for children, further suggests that these stories may provide information for young adolescents about worlds they will be expected to enter.

The other one-half of all stories told around the family dinner table were of the familial past, both shared family stories, stories of long ago holidays, vacations and outings, and also intergenerational narratives, stories about when the parents themselves were growing up, and what their childhood experiences were like. All families told at least one intergenerational narrative around the dinner table, and most told several. Somewhat surprisingly, children brought up these intergenerational stories as topics of conversation as often as parents did, and children contributed as much to the telling of these stories as did parents, indicating that these stories were told previously, and that adolescents were interested in the stories and the telling of them. Family reminiscing around the dinner table was generally related to child well-being; families that told more stories overall had children with fewer internalizing (depression, anxiety) and externalizing (anger, aggression) behaviors than families that told fewer stories, and these effects were especially strong for intergenerational stories. Families that told more inter-generational stories around the dinner table had children who showed higher levels of self-esteem and few behavior problems (Bohanek et al., 2009). Intergenerational stories may be a particularly potent context, providing children and adolescents with more extended historical timelines within which to place their own stories, as well as providing models of how to live a life, as we saw in Dave's narrative earlier.

Several studies have now explicitly asked US adolescents and emerging adults to tell stories they know about their parents' childhoods, asking for any story they might know, or specifically for stories about a time their parent was proud, or ashamed, or an event that defines who their parent is as a person (see Merrill & Fivush, 2016, for a review). Across these studies three major findings emerged. First, virtually all adolescents studied provided stories about both their mothers' and fathers' childhoods, stories that adolescents reported being told by the parent to the child, indicating that this is a common family conver-sational interaction (Merrill et al., 2019). Second, there are individual differ-ences in how adolescents tell these stories. Adolescents who tell more elaborated intergenerational stories that take the perspective of the parent, again as seen in Dave's narrative of what his mother was thinking and feeling during the narrated event, show higher levels of well-being (Fivush, 2019c) and more secure attachment relationships (Zaman & Fivush, 2013). These findings have now been replicated across three New Zealand samples: the indigenous Maori population that values oral traditions and family ancestry, Chinese New Zealanders, who are a more communally oriented culture, and New Zealand Europeans, who are a more autonomously oriented culture (Reese et al., 2017). Adolescents in all three groups easily tell intergenerational stories, but Maori and Chinese adolescents include more explicit connections between self and parent, and reported that parents told these stories more for teaching life lessons than did European adolescents. Thus, adolescent's own life stories are embed-ded in larger family stories that are themselves embedded in larger cultural contexts. And knowing these intergenerational stories provides predictive power for adolescent's self-esteem and well-being across the cultures studied (Chen et al., 2021).

5.3.2 Culture, Media, and Autobiographical Memory

Earlier in this Element, I discussed how culturally mediated master narratives and life scripts provide frameworks for organizing and expressing personal memories, and how cultural frameworks are communicated in the larger culture through culturally shared stories and master narrative arcs. Children likely learn life script and canonical narrative arcs both through maternal scaffolding of life stories, family reminiscing, and intergenerational narratives and also through canonical cultural narratives as displayed in media, such as books, movies, and social media platforms. There is some suggestion that adolescents look to novels and films for models of how to live a life (Breen et al., 2017) and use diary writing to explore different ways of being in the world (Harbus, 2011). This is an intriguing question for future research, and developmental psychology would benefit from taking a more interdisciplinary approach, drawing on work in sociology, literary studies, media studies, and cultural studies, to explore connections between cultural templates and individual life stories. Examining connections between and among culturally provided canonical narrative forms and personal life narratives could fruitfully illuminate how the individual and culture meet at the intersection of narratives.

By late adolescence, individuals across cultures construct a chronologically and causally organized life story that weaves discrete, recurring, and extended personal memories into a coherent personal timeline linked through a subjective perspective, what the individual was thinking and feeling then and now, creating an autobiographical consciousness (Fivush et al., 2011; Nelson & Fivush, 2020). The canonical narrative forms for constructing a life, and the various experiences that make up this life, infuse local and cultural interactions, shaping and being shaped by individual experience. This is a remarkable human developmental process.

6 Conclusions and Future Directions

This Element began with a broad, and perhaps bold, claim: autobiographical memory is the glue that integrates our experiences into a cohesive whole through narrative meaning-making and creates a sense of continuity and coherence through an autobiographical consciousness that defines each of us as a unique self. In support of this claim, I reviewed how autobiographical memory cannot simply be defined as a subpart of a broader memory system or process; without senses of self, other, and mind, memories would not be autobiographical, and thus autobiographical memory by definition breaks the boundaries of "memory" as typically defined. Furthermore, sense of self, other, and mind are not possible outside of a culturally mediated system that allows individuals to interact in the world in ways that highlight mind of self and other, and this is done through narrative. Outside of canonical narrative forms, it is difficult to imagine how an individual could come to form a sense of self as continuous through time, with both stable and changing inner states, that may be the same and/or different than others. This form of subjectivity, which we see developing across the narratives presented in this Element, seems to be uniquely human and is the basis of an autobiographical consciousness, a consciousness of self experiencing and evaluating through time and in relation to others. It is in this sense that culture and narrative are tightly linked; both define what a life should look like and how a life should be lived. These canonical cultural narrative forms are expressed in everyday reminiscing conversations beginning in the preschool years, becoming more complex, temporally extended and self-evaluative and defining through adolescence. Several conclusions emerge from this review and analysis, some explicit and some implicit throughout this Element.

First, stemming from the larger discussion of memory as a dynamic, reconstructive process, autobiographical memory, or memories, or narratives, must be conceptualized as dynamic processes, both across short spans of time and across larger developmental timespans (Fivush et al., 2017). Whereas the research has demonstrated that more elaborative maternal reminiscing early in development provides a foundation for more elaborated autobiographical memory, narratives, and understanding of mind across development, it is also the case that every reminiscing conversation is itself unique. Every time an event is brought to mind, somewhat different patterns of activation occur, recalling many of the same details but also adding, deleting, and inferring other details. The claim is not that maternal elaborative reminiscing leads to specific stable autobiographical memories and narratives, but rather that maternal elaborative reminiscing inculcates a style of reminiscing, such that children of more elaborative mothers come to perceive, evaluate, and recall their experiences in more elaborative ways. These children develop more elaborated autobiographical processes.

Moreover, development of autobiographical memories and narratives occurs gradually across childhood and adolescence (and across adulthood as well; McAdams, 2008). As a dynamic process, autobiographical memories and narratives may become more or less stable at particular points in developmental time, depending on how and why these experiences are being recalled. In the moment, stability and/or change of autobiographical narratives may depend on current goals and contexts (e.g., Conway & Pleydell-Pearce, 2000), and across time, stability and/or change in autobiographical narratives may depend on the developmental tasks one is facing. For example, adolescents tell narratives dripping with identity issues, whereas middle-age adults foreground issues of generativity and their life legacy (McAdams, 2008). Differences in narrative themes depending on age highlights the interweaving developments of autobiographical memory and self. Autobiographical memory and self cannot be disentangled. Both the stories that we tell and how we tell them will be molded by the local and developmental context, and these stories will both construct and define self dynamically over time.

Furthermore, in a fully transactional process, autobiographical memory is memory of self, and self is at least partly culturally constructed through canonically mediated narratives of what a self is and how to live a life. The argument is not that our autobiographical memories are completely imposed or constrained by cultural frameworks, but that as we construct narratives of self, we are at the interface of culture and individual. Cultures provide the tools, but individuals can adapt those tools in new ways, although this may take substantial developmental or historical time. The perspective of culture as being defined at least partly through the canonical narrative frameworks for world-making further suggests that studying narrative is, itself, a study of culture. When we study individual autobiographical memory, we are simultaneously studying cultural processes. Explicating the cultural analysis in all our research is essential.

This approach also shapes the kinds of questions that research still needs to address, and how to address them. For example, gender remains a paradox in the autobiographical memory literature. Girls and women narrate in more detailed, emotionally expressive, and relationally oriented ways than do boys and men, at least in most studies and in most cultures studied thus far (Grysman & Hudson, 2013). Mothers and fathers seem to differ from each other but do not differ in how they reminisce with daughters compared to sons. How and why do we see gender differences in personal narratives? And when do we not see them? How might we delve deeper into context to answer this question? And how and when does gender identity matter versus biological sex? Grysman and colleagues (Grysman & Denney, 2017; Grysman et al., 2016; Grysman et al., 2017) have begun to explore these questions, but answers remain elusive. The patterns of narrative similarities and differences by gender confirm that autobiographical narratives are dynamic, evolving, and context-sensitive – so gender may not be an explanatory variable at all, but rather one part of a dynamically changing system. Gender, itself, might be a process at least partly constructed through narrative (Fivush & Grysman, 2019).

Similarly, we still do not really know why some mothers are more elaborative when reminiscing than others. There is remarkable consistency in the dimension of elaboration as critical in many cultures studied in relation to multiple child outcomes, yet we still do not have a full explanation for why some mothers may be more elaborative than others. And most of this research has focused on the preschool years, as coherent autobiographical memories emerge. More research on how this process proceeds developmentally, especially in adolescence as individuals begin to differentiate from family and fashion their own identity is needed (e.g., Habermas, 2011; McLean, 2015). One of the problems we may face in this research is trying to identify maternal characteristics and child characteristics as independent, when it is more likely that mothers and children engage in ongoing dialectally related cascades of behaviors over time (Reese et al., 1993). How to characterize the complexity of developmental processes in context is one that faces the entire field of developmental science and challenges some of our most cherished methodologies (Sameroff, 2010). Often our experimental tasks come to define the phenomenon we are interested in, but we lose the actual phenomenon by focusing on the methodological task instead of the everyday lived practices of children within families and communities. Deeper qualitative analyses would be beneficial in this regard.

Many additional questions emerge from this Element, but certain reasonably firm conclusions emerge as well. Autobiographical memory is the heart of who we are. We savor our most cherished memories in moments of reflection, and we share our selves through our stories in everyday conversations, celebrating major accomplishments, grieving our losses, and just communicating the texture of our lives to and with others. Memories, themselves, are complex processes of ongoing dynamic reactivations, and the ways in which memories and selves become intertwined constitute a long developmental process that unfolds in everyday culturally mediated reminiscing conversations within the family embedded within culturally canonical narrative tools for making selves and making worlds. Our ability to construct a coherent evaluative timeline of our personal experiences, our life story, and our autobiographical consciousness is a uniquely human achievement that affords meaning and purpose in human lives. But it is not an individual achievement. Autobiographical memories are formed and re-formed in the narrative interactions that shape how and what we remember each time we recall and as we recall over time. The individual self and culture meet at the point where stories are told.

References

Alba, J. W., & Hasher, L. (1983). Is memory schematic? *Psychological Bulletin*, *93*(2), 203–231. https://doi.org/10.1037/0033-2909.93.2.203.

Andrews, R., & Van Bergen, P. (2020). Characteristics of educators' talk about decontextualised events. *Australasian Journal of Early Childhood*, *45*(4), 362–376. https://doi.org/10.1177/1836939120966080.

Arendell, T. (2000). Conceiving and investigating motherhood: The decade's scholarship. *Journal of Marriage and Family*, *62*(4), 1192–1207. https://doi .org/10.1111/j.1741-3737.2000.01192.x.

Artioli, F., Reese, E., & Hayne, H. (2015). Benchmarking the past: Children's early memories and maternal reminiscing as a function of family structure. *Journal of Applied Research in Memory and Cognition*, *4*(2), 136–143. https://doi.org/10.1016/j.jarmac.2015.04.002.

Ashburn-Nardo, L. (2017). Parenthood as a moral imperative? Moral outrage and the stigmatization of voluntarily childfree women and men. *Sex Roles*, *76* (5), 393–401. https://doi.org/10.1007/s11199-016-0606-1.

Astington, J. W., & Baird, J. A. (Eds.). (2005). *Why language matters for theory of mind*. Oxford: Oxford University Press. https://doi.org/10.1093/acprof: oso/9780195159912.001.0001.

Aznar, A., & Tenenbaum, H. R. (2020). Gender comparisons in mother-child emotion talk: A meta-analysis. *Sex Roles*, *82*(3), 155–162. https://doi.org/10 .1007/s11199-019-01042-y.

Baddeley, A. (1988). But what the hell is it for? In Gruneberg, M., Morris, P., & Skyes, R. (Eds.). *Practical aspect of memory: Current research and issues* (pp. 3–18), Chicester: Wiley .

Barclay, C. R. (1986). Schematization of autobiographical memory. In D. C. Rubin (Ed.). *Autobiographical memory* (pp. 82–99), New York: Cambridge University Press. https://doi.org/10.1017/CBO9780511558313 .010.

Barnes, H. E. (1998). *The story I tell myself: A venture in existentialist auto-biography*. Chicago, IL: University of Chicago Press. https://doi.org/10.7208/ chicago/9780226037349.001.0001.

Bartlett, F. C. (1932). *Remembering: A study in experimental and social psych-ology*. New York: Cambridge University Press.

Bauer, P. J. (2015). Development of episodic and autobiographical memory: The importance of remembering forgetting. *Developmental Review*, *38*, 146–166. https://doi.org/10.1016/j.dr.2015.07.011.

Bauer, P. J., & Larkina, M. (2019). Predictors of age-related and individual variability in autobiographical memory in childhood. *Memory, 27*(1), 63–78. https://doi.org/10.1080/09658211.2017.1381267.

Bauer, P. J., & Leventon, J. S. (2013). Memory for one-time experiences in the second year of life: Implications for the status of episodic memory. *Infancy, 18*(5), 755–781. https://doi.org/10.1111/infa.12005.

Berntsen, D., & Rubin, D. C. (2004). Cultural life scripts structure recall from autobiographical memory. *Memory & Cognition, 32*(3), 427–442. https://doi .org/10.3758/BF03195836.

Bird, A., & Reese, E. (2006). Emotional reminiscing and the development of an autobiographical self. *Developmental Psychology, 42*(4), 613. https://doi.org/ 10.1037/0012-1649.42.4.613.

Bird, A., Reese, E., & Tripp, G. (2006). Parent–child talk about past emotional events: Associations with child temperament and goodness-of-fit. *Journal of Cognition and Development, 7*(2), 189–210. https://doi.org/10.1207/s15327 647jcd0702_3.

Bluck, S., Alea, N., Habermas, T., & Rubin, D. C. (2005). A tale of three functions: The self-reported uses of autobiographical memory. *Social Cognition, 23*(1), 91–117. https://doi.org/10.1521/soco.23.1.91.59198.

Bohanek, J. G., Fivush, R., Zaman, W. et al. (2009). Narrative interaction in family dinnertime conversations. *Merrill-Palmer Quarterly, 55*(4), 488–515. https://doi.org/10.1353/mpq.0.0031.

Bohn, A., & Berntsen, D. (2008). Life story development in childhood: The development of life story abilities and the acquisition of cultural life scripts from late middle childhood to adolescence. *Developmental Psychology, 44* (4), 1135. https://doi.org/10.1037/0012-1649.44.4.1135.

Boland, A. M., Haden, C. A., & Ornstein, P. A. (2003). Boosting children's memory by training mothers in the use of an elaborative conversational style as an event unfolds. *Journal of Cognition and Development, 4*(1), 39–65. http://doi.org/10.1080/15248372.2003.9669682.

Bornstein, M. H. (2013). *Cultural approaches to parenting.* New York: Psychology Press. https://doi.org/10.4324/9780203772676.

Boyd, B. (2018). The evolution of stories: From mimesis to language, from fact to fiction. *Wiley Interdisciplinary Reviews: Cognitive Science, 9*(1), e1444. https://doi.org/10.1002/wcs.1444.

Bransford, J. D., Barclay, J. R., & Franks, J. J. (1972). Sentence memory: A constructive versus interpretive approach. *Cognitive Psychology, 3*(2), 193–209. https://doi.org/10.1016/0010-0285(72)90003-5.

Breen, A. V., McLean, K. C., Cairney, K., & McAdams, D. P. (2017). Movies, books, and identity: Exploring the narrative ecology of the self. *Qualitative Psychology, 4*(3), 243–259. https://doi.org/10.1037/qup0000059.

Bretherton, I. (1995). A communication perspective on attachment relationships and internal working models. *Monographs of the Society for Research in Child Development, 60*(2–3), 310–329. https://doi.org/10.1111/j.1540-5834.1995.tb00220.x.

Brockmeier, J. (2015). *Beyond the archive: Memory, narrative, and the autobiographical process.* Oxford University Press. https://doi.org/10.1093/acprof:oso/9780199861569.001.0001.

Brockmeier, J. (2019). Memory, narrative, and the consequences. *Topics in Cognitive Science, 11*(4), 821–824. https://doi.org/10.1111/tops.12412.

Bruner, J. (1990). *Acts of meaning.* Cambridge, MA: Harvard University Press.

Bruner, J. (1991). The narrative construction of reality. *Critical Inquiry, 18,* 1–21. https://doi.org/10.1086/448619.

Buckner, J. P., & Fivush IV, R. (2000). Gendered themes in family reminiscing. *Memory, 8*(6), 401–412. https://doi.org/10.1080/09658210050156859.

Budds, K. (2013). A critical discursive analysis of "older" motherhood. Unpublished Ph.D. thesis, University of Huddersfield.

Burkart, J. M., Hrdy, S. B., & Van Schaik, C. P. (2009). Cooperative breeding and human cognitive evolution. *Evolutionary Anthropology: Issues, News, and Reviews: Issues, News, and Reviews, 18*(5), 175–186. https://doi.org/10.1002/evan.20222.

Cabrera, N. J., Volling, B. L., & Barr, R. (2018). Fathers are parents, too! Widening the lens on parenting for children's development. *Child Development Perspectives, 12*(3), 152–157. https://doi.org/10.1111/cdep.12275.

Call, J., & Tomasello, M. (2008). Does the chimpanzee have a theory of mind? 30 years later. *Trends in Cognitive Sciences, 12*(5), 187–192. https://doi.org/10.1016/j.tics.2008.02.010.

Canada, K. L., Pathman, T., & Riggins, T. (2020). Longitudinal development of memory for temporal order in early to middle childhood. *The Journal of Genetic Psychology, 181*(4), 237–254. https://doi.org/10.1080/00221325.2020.1741504.

Caspe, M., & Melzi, G. (2008). Cultural variations in mother-child narrative discourse style. In A. McCabe, A. L. Bailey, & G. Melzi (Eds.), *Spanish-language narration and literacy: Culture, cognition, and emotion* (pp. 6–33), Cambridge University Press. https://doi.org/10.1017/CBO9780511815669.004

Chen, Y., Cullen, E., Fivush, R., Wang, Q., & Reese, E. (2021). Mother, father, and I: A cross-cultural investigation of adolescents' intergenerational narratives and well-being. *Journal of Applied Research in Memory and Cognition, 10*(1), 55–64. https://doi.org/10.1016/j.jarmac.2020.08.011.

Clayton, N. S., Bussey, T. J., & Dickinson, A. (2003). Can animals recall the past and plan for the future? *Nature Reviews Neuroscience, 4*(8), 685–691. https://doi.org/10.1038/nrn1180.

Conroy, R., & Salmon, K. (2006). Talking about parts of a past experience: The impact of discussion style and event structure on memory for discussed and nondiscussed information. *Journal of Experimental Child Psychology, 95*(4), 278–297. https://doi.org/10.1016/j.jecp.2006.06.001.

Conway, M. A., & Pleydell-Pearce, C. W. (2000). The construction of autobiographical memories in the self-memory system. *Psychological Review, 107* (2), 261–288. https://doi.org/10.1037/0033-295X.107.2.261.

Conway, M. A., Singer, J. A., & Tagini, A. (2004). The self and autobiographical memory: Correspondence and coherence. *Social Cognition, 22*(5:Special issue), 491–529. https://doi.org/10.1521/soco.22.5.491.50768.

Cristofaro, T. N., & Tamis-LeMonda, C. S. (2008). Lessons in mother-child and father-child personal narratives in Latino families. In A. McCabe, A. L. Bailey, & G. Melzi (Eds.), *Spanish-language narration and literacy: Culture, cognition, and emotion* (pp. 54–91). Cambridge University Press. https://doi.org/10.1017/CBO9780511815669.006

Crystal, J. D. (2010). Episodic-like memory in animals. *Behavioural Brain Research, 215*(2), 235–243. https://doi.org/10.1016/j.bbr.2010.03.005.

Damasio, A. (2012). *Self comes to mind: Constructing the conscious brain.* New York: Vintage.

De Brigard, F. (2014). The nature of memory traces. *Philosophy Compass, 9*(6), 402–414. https://doi.org/10.1111/phc3.12133.

De Leersnyder, J., Boiger, M., & Mesquita, B. (2015). Emerging trends: Cultural differences in emotion. *Emerging Trends in the Social Sciences,* 1–22. https://doi.org/10.1002/9781118900772.etrds0060

Donald, M. (2001). *A mind so rare: The evolution of human consciousness.* New York: W. W. Norton.

Dor, D. (2014). The instruction of imagination: language and its evolution as a communication strategy. In D. Dor, C. Knight & J. Lewis (Eds.). *The social origins of language* (pp. 105–128). Oxford: Oxford University Press. https://doi.org/10.1093/acprof:oso/9780199665327.003.0009

Dudai, Y., & Edelson, M. G. (2016). Personal memory: Is it personal, is it memory?. *Memory Studies, 9*(3), 275–283. https://doi.org/10.1177/175069 8016645234

Ebbinghaus, H. (2013). Memory: A contribution to experimental psychology. *Annals of Neurosciences, 20*(4), 155. https://doi.org/10.5214/ans.0972.7531 .200408

Erikson, E. H. (1968). *Identity: Youth and crisis* (No. 7). WW Norton & company.

Etzion-Carasso, A., & Oppenheim, D. (2000). Open mother–pre-schooler communication: Relations with early secure attachment. *Attachment & Human Development, 2*(3), 347–370. https://doi.org/10.5214/ans.0972.7531.200408

Farrant, K., & Reese, E. (2000). Maternal style and children's participation in reminiscing: Stepping stones in children's autobiographical memory development. *Journal of Cognition and Development, 1*, 193–225. https://doi.org/10.1207/S15327647JCD010203

Faulkner, W. (1951). Requiem for a nun. New York: Vintage International.

Fivush, R. (2007). Maternal reminiscing style and children's developing understanding of self and emotion. *Clinical Social Work Journal, 35*(1), 37–46. https://doi.org/10.1007/s10615-006-0065-1

Fivush, R. (2010a). Speaking silence: The social construction of voice and silence in cultural and autobiographical narratives. *Memory, 18*, 88–98. https://doi.org/10.1080/09658210903029404

Fivush, R. (2010b). The development of autobiographical memory. *Annual Review of Psychology, 62*, 2.1–2.24. https://doi.org/10.1146/annurev.psych.121208.131702

Fivush, R. (2019a). *Family narratives and the development of the autobiographical self: Social and cultural perspectives on autobiographical memory.* New York: Routledge. https://doi.org/10.4324/9780429029158

Fivush. R. (2019b). "A life without stories is no life at all": How stories create selves. *Evolutionary Studies in Imaginative Culture, 3*(1), 41–44. https://doi.org/10.26613/esic.3.1.116

Fivush, R. (2019c). Sociocultural developmental approaches to autobiographical memory. *Applied Cognitive Psychology, 33*(4), 489–497. https://doi.org/10.1002/acp.3512

Fivush, R., Booker, J. A., & Graci, M. (2017). Ongoing narrative meaning-making within events and across the lifespan. *Imagination, Cognition and Personality, 37*, 127–152. https://doi.org/10.1177/0276236617733824

Fivush, R., & Graci, M. E. (2017). Autobiographical memory. In J. Wixted (Ed.). *Learning and memory: A comprehensive reference 2nd edition.* Elsevier. https://doi.org/10.1016/B978-0-12-809324-5.21046-8

Fivush, R., & Grysman, A. (2019). Emotion and gender in personal narratives. In S.E. Pritzker, J. Fenigsen & J.M. Wilce (Eds.). *The Routledge handbook of language and emotion* (pp. 344–359). New York: Routledge. https://doi.org/10.4324/9780367855093-20

Fivush, R., & Grysman, A. (2022). Narrative and gender as mutually constituted meaning-making systems. *Memory, Mind & Media, 1*, 1–14. https://doi.org/10.1017/mem.2021.4

Fivush, R., Habermas, T., Waters, T. E., & Zaman, W. (2011). The making of autobiographical memory: Intersections of culture, narratives and identity. *International Journal of Psychology, 46*(5), 321–345. https://doi.org/10.1080/00207594.2011.596541

Fivush, R., Haden, C. A., & Reese, E. (2006). Elaborating on elaborations: Maternal reminiscing style and children's socioemotional outcome. *Child Development, 77,* 1568–1588. https://doi.org/10.1111/j.1467-8624.2006.00960.x

Fivush, R., Marin, K., McWilliams, K., & Bohanek, J. G. (2009). Family reminiscing style: Parent gender and emotional focus in relation to child well-being. *Journal of Cognition and Development, 10*(3), 210–235. https://doi.org/10.1080/15248370903155866

Fivush. R., & Merrill, N. (2016). An ecological systems approach to family narratives. *Memory Studies, 9*(3), 305–314. https://doi.org/10.1177/1750698016645264

Fivush, R., & Nelson, K. (2006). Parent–child reminiscing locates the self in the past. *British Journal of Developmental Psychology, 24*(1), 235–251. https://doi.org/10.1348/026151005X57747

Fivush, R., Reese, E., & Booker, J. A. (2019). Developmental foundations of the narrative author in early mother-child reminiscing. In D. McAdams (Ed.). *Handbook on personality development* (pp. 399–417). New York: Cambridge University Press.

Fivush, R., & Vasudeva, A. (2002). Remembering to relate: Socioemotional correlates of mother-child reminiscing. *Journal of Cognition and Development, 3*(1), 73–90. https://doi.org/10.1207/S15327647JCD0301_5

Fivush, R., & Wang, Q. (2005). Emotion talk in mother-child conversations of the shared past: The effects of culture, gender, and event valence. *Journal of Cognition and Development, 6*(4), 489–506. https://doi.org/10.1207/s15327647jcd0604_3

Fivush, R., & Waters, T. E. A. (2019). Development and organization of autobiographical memory form and function. In John Mace (Ed.). *The organization and structure of autobiographical memory* (pp.52–71). Oxford: Oxford University Press. https://doi.org/10.1093/oso/9780198784845.003.0004

Fivush, R., & Zaman, W. (2014). Gender, subjective perspective, and autobiographical consciousness. In P. J. Bauer & R. Fivush (Eds.). *The Wiley handbook on the development of children's memory* (pp. 586–604). New York: Wiley Blackwell. https://doi.org/10.1002/9781118597705.ch25

Friedman, W. J. (2003). The development of a differentiated sense of the past and the future. *Advances in Child Development and Behavior, 31*, 229–269. https://doi.org/10.1016/S0065-2407(03)31006-7

Frith, C. D., & Frith, U. (2007). Social cognition in humans. *Current Biology, 17* (16), R724–R732. https://doi.org/10.1016/j.cub.2007.05.068

Ghavami, N., Katsiaficas, D., & Rogers, L. O. (2016). Toward an intersectional approach in developmental science: The role of race, gender, sexual orientation, and immigrant status. *Advances in Child Development and Behavior, 50*, 31–73. https://doi.org/10.1016/bs.acdb.2015.12.001

Ghetti, S., & Bunge, S. A. (2012). Neural changes underlying the development of episodic memory during middle childhood. *Developmental Cognitive Neuroscience, 2*(4), 381–395. https://doi.org/10.1016/j.dcn.2012.05.002

Goodman, N. (1978). *Ways of worldmaking* (Vol. 51). Cambridge: Hackett.

Gotlib, A. (2016). "But you would be the best mother": Unwomen, counterstories, and the motherhood mandate. *Journal of Bioethical Inquiry, 13*(2), 327–347. https://doi.org/10.1007/s11673-016-9699-z

Grysman, A., & Denney, A. (2017). Gender, experimenter gender and medium of report influence the content of autobiographical memory report. *Memory, 25*(1), 132–145. https://doi.org/10.1007/s11673-016-9699-z

Grysman, A., Fivush, R., Merrill, N. A., & Graci, M. (2016). The influence of gender and gender typicality on autobiographical memory across event types and age groups. *Memory & Cognition, 44*(6), 856–868. https://doi.org/10.3758/s13421-016-0610-2

Grysman, A., & Hudson, J. A. (2013). Gender differences in autobiographical memory: Developmental and methodological considerations. *Developmental Review, 33*(3), 239–272. https://doi.org/10.1016/j.dr.2013.07.004

Grysman, A., Merrill, N., & Fivush, R. (2017). Emotion, gender, and gender typical identity in autobiographical memory. *Memory, 25*(3), 289–297. https://doi.org/10.1080/09658211.2016.1168847

Habermas, T. (2011). Autobiographical reasoning: Arguing and narrating from a biographical perspective. *New Directions for Child and Adolescent Development, 2011*(131), 1–17. https://doi.org/10.1002/cd.285

Habermas, T., & Bluck, S. (2000). Getting a life: The emergence of the life story in adolescence. *Psychological Bulletin, 126*(5), 748. https://doi.org/10.1037/0033-2909.126.5.748

Habermas, T., & de Silveira, C. (2008). The development of global coherence in life narratives across adolescence: Temporal, causal, and thematic aspects. *Developmental Psychology, 44*(3), 707. https://doi.org/10.1037/0012-1649.44.3.707

Habermas, T., & Köber, C. (2014). Autobiographical reasoning is constitutive for narrative identity: The role of the life story for personal continuity. In K. McLean & M. Seyd (Eds.). *The Oxford handbook of identity development* (p. 149). Oxford: Oxford University Press. https://doi.org/10.1093/oxfordhb/9780199936564.013.010

Habermas, T., Negele, A., & Mayer, F. B. (2010). "Honey, you're jumping about"—Mothers' scaffolding of their children's and adolescents' life narration. *Cognitive Development, 25*(4), 339–351. https://doi.org/10.1016/j.cogdev.2010.08.004

Habermas, T., & Paha, C. (2001). The development of coherence in adolescents' life narratives. *Narrative Inquiry, 11*(1), 35–54. https://doi.org/10.1075/ni.11.1.02hab

Haden, C. A., Ornstein, P. A., Eckerman, C. O., & Didow, S. M. (2001). Mother–child conversational interactions as events unfold: Linkages to subsequent remembering. *Child Development, 72*(4), 1016–1031. https://doi.org/10.1111/1467-8624.00332

Hall, H. K., Millear, P. M., Summers, M. J., & Isbel, B. (2021). Longitudinal research on perspective taking in adolescence: A systematic review. *Adolescent Research Review, 6*(2), 125–150. https://doi.org/10.1007/s40894-021-00150-9

Hammack, P. L. (2011). Narrative and the politics of meaning. *Narrative Inquiry, 21*(2), 311–318. https://doi.org/10.1075/ni.21.2.09ham

Harbus, A. (2011). Exposure to life-writing as an impact on autobiographical memory. *Memory Studies, 4*(2), 206–220. https://doi.org/10.1177/1750698010389571

Hassabis, D., & Maguire, E. A. (2007). Deconstructing episodic memory with construction. *Trends in Cognitive Sciences, 11*(7), 299–306. https://doi.org/10.1016/j.tics.2007.05.001

Hirst, W., & Echteroff, G. (2012). Remembering in conversations: The social sharing and reshaping of memories. *Annual Review of Psychology, 63*, 55–79. https://doi.org/10.1146/annurev-psych-120710-100340

Hutto, D. (2007). Narrative and understanding persons. *Royal Institute of Philosophy Supplements, 60*, 1–15. https://doi.org/10.1017/S135824610000009589

Jahoda, G. (2012). Critical reflections on some recent definitions of "culture". *Culture & Psychology, 18*(3), 289–303. https://doi.org/10.1177/1354067X12446229

James, W. (1890). *The principles of psychology.* New York: Dover. https://doi.org/10.1037/10538-000

Kerrick, M. R., & Henry, R. L. (2017). "Totally in love": Evidence of a master narrative for how new mothers should feel about their babies. *Sex Roles, 76* (1–2), 1–16. https://doi.org/10.1007/s11199-016-0666-2

Köber, C., & Habermas, T. (2017). Development of temporal macrostructure in life narratives across the lifespan. *Discourse Processes, 54*(2), 143–162. https://doi.org/10.1080/0163853X.2015.1105619

Kulkofsky, S., Wang, Q., & Koh, J. B. (2009). Functions of memory sharing and mother-child reminiscing behaviors: Individual and cultural variations. *Journal of Cognition and Development, 10* (1–2), 92–114. https://doi.org/10.1080/15248370903041231

Labov, W. (2010). Oral narratives of personal experience. *Cambridge Encyclopedia of the Language Sciences*, 546–548. Cambridge.

Laible, D., Panfile Murphy, T., & Augustine, M. (2013). Constructing emotional and relational understanding: The role of mother–child reminiscing about negatively valenced events. *Social Development, 22*(2), 300–318. https://doi.org/10.1111/sode.12022

Langley, H. A., Coffman, J. L., & Ornstein, P. A. (2017). The socialization of children's memory: Linking maternal conversational style to the development of children's autobiographical and deliberate memory skills. *Journal of Cognition and Development, 18*(1), 63–86. https://doi.org/10.1080/15248372.2015.1135800

Lawson, M., Valentino, K., Speidel, R., McDonnell, C. G., & Cummings, E. M. (2020). Reduced autobiographical memory specificity among maltreated preschoolers: The indirect effect of neglect through maternal reminiscing. *Child Development, 91*(1), 271–288. https://doi.org/10.1111/cdev.13153

Loftus, E. F. (2003). Make-believe memories. *American Psychologist, 58*(11), 867. https://doi.org/10.1037/0003-066X.58.11.867

Mandler, J. M., & Cánovas, C. P. (2014). On defining image schemas. *Language and Cognition, 6*(4), 510–532. https://doi.org/10.1017/langcog.2014.14

McAdams, D. P. (1992). Unity and purpose in human lives: The emergence of identity as a life story. In R. A. Zucker, A. I. Rabin, J. Aronoff & S. J. Frank (Eds.). *Personality structure in the life course* (pp. 323–375). New York: Springer.

McAdams, D. P. (2004). The redemptive self: Narrative identity in America today. In D. R. Beike, J. M. Lampinen, & D. A. Behrend (Eds.). *The self and memory* (pp. 95–116). New York: Psychology Press.

McAdams, D. P. (2008). Personal narratives and the life story. In John, Robins & Pervin (Eds.). *Handbook of personality: Theory and research (3rd edition)* (pp. 242–262). New York: Willford Press

McAdams, D. P. (2019). "First we invented stories, then they changed us": The evolution of narrative identity. *Evolutionary Studies in Imaginative Culture*, *3*(1), 1–18. https://doi.org/10.26613/esic.3.1.110

McGuigan, F., & Salmon, K. (2004). The time to talk: The influence of the timing of adult–child talk on children's event memory. *Child Development*, *75*(3), 669–686. https://doi.org/10.1111/j.1467-8624.2004.00700.x

McLean, K. (2015). *The co-authored self*. New York: Oxford University Press. https://doi.org/10.1093/acprof:oso/9780199995745.001.0001

McLean, K. C., & Syed, M. (2015). Personal, master, and alternative narratives: An integrative framework for understanding identity development in context. *Human Development*, *58*(6), 318–349. https://doi.org/10.1159/000445817

Melzi, G. (2000). Cultural variations in the construction of personal narratives: Central American and European American mothers' elicitation styles. *Discourse Processes*, *30*(2), 153–177. https://doi.org/10.1207/S15326950 DP3002_04

Merrill, N., Booker, J. A., & Fivush, R. (2019). Functions of parental intergenerational narratives told by young people. *Topics in Cognitive Science*, *11*(4), 752–773. https://doi.org/10.1111/tops.12356

Merrill, N., & Fivush, R. (2016). Intergenerational narratives and identity across development. *Developmental Review*, *40*, 72–92. https://doi.org/10 .1016/j.dr.2016.03.001

Merrill, N., Gallo, E., & Fivush, R. (2015). Gender differences in family dinnertime conversations. *Discourse Processes*, *52*(7), 533–558. https://doi .org/10.1080/0163853X.2014.958425

Miller, P. J., Potts, R., Fung, H., Hoogstra, L., & Mintz, J. (1990). Narrative practices and the social construction of self in childhood. *American Ethnologist*, *17*(2), 292–311. https://doi.org/10.1525/ae.1990.17.2.02a00060

Miller, T. (2005). *Making sense of motherhood: A narrative approach*. Cambridge: Cambridge University Press. https://doi.org/10.1017/ CBO9780511489501

Mistry, J., & Dutta, R. (2015). Human development and culture. In R. M. Lerner (Ed.). *Handbook of child psychology and developmental science* (7th ed., Vol 1, pp. 369–406). New York: John Wiley. https://doi.org/10.1002/9781118963418 .childpsy110

Neisser, U. (2014). *Cognitive psychology: Classic edition*. Psychology Press. https://doi.org/10.4324/9781315736174

Neisser, U., & Hyman, I. (2000). *Memory observed: Remembering in natural contexts*. New York: Macmillan.

Nelson K. (1986). *Generalized event representations*. Mahway, NJ: Erlbaum.

Nelson, K., & Fivush, R. (2004). The emergence of autobiographical memory: A social cultural developmental model. *Psychological Review, 111*(2), 486–511. https://doi.org/10.1037/0033-295X.111.2.486

Nelson, K., & Fivush, R. (2020). The development of autobiographical memory, autobiographical narratives, and autobiographical consciousness. *Psychological Reports, 123*(1), 71–96. https://doi.org/10.1177/0033294119852574

Newcombe, R., & Reese, E. (2004). Evaluations and orientations in mother–child narratives as a function of attachment security: A longitudinal investigation. *International Journal of Behavioral Development, 28*(3), 230–245. https://doi.org/10.1080/01650250344000460

Oppenheim, D., Koren-Karie, N., & Sagi-Schwartz, A. (2007). Emotion dialogues between mothers and children at 4.5 and 7.5 years: Relations with children's attachment at 1 year. *Child Development, 78*(1), 38–52. https://doi.org/10.1111/j.1467-8624.2007.00984.x

Ottsen, C. L., & Berntsen, D. (2014). The cultural life script of Qatar and across cultures: Effects of gender and religion. *Memory, 22*(4), 390–407. https://doi.org/10.1080/09658211.2013.795598

Pasupathi, M. (2001). The social construction of the personal past and its implications for adult development. *Psychological Bulletin, 127*(5), 651. https://doi.org/10.1037/0033-2909.127.5.651

Pasupathi, M., Mansour, E., & Brubaker, J. R. (2007). Developing a life story: Constructing relations between self and experience in autobiographical narratives. *Human Development, 50*(2–3), 85–110. https://doi.org/10.1159/000100939

Perlin, J. D., & Fivush, R. (2021). Revisiting redemption: A life span developmental account of the functions of narrative redemption. *Human Development, 65*(1), 23–42. https://doi.org/10.1159/000514357

Peterson, C., Jesso, B., & McCabe, A. (1999). Encouraging narratives in preschoolers: An intervention study. *Journal of Child Language, 26*(1), 49–67. https://doi.org/10.1017/S0305000998003651

Povinelli, D. J. (2001). The self: Elevated in consciousness and extended in time. In C. Moore & K. Lemmon (Eds.). *The self in time* (pp. 83–104). Psychology Press. https://doi.org/10.4324/9781410600684-9

Raikes, H. A., & Thompson, R. A. (2008). Conversations about emotion in high-risk dyads. *Attachment & Human Development, 10*(4), 359–377. https://doi.org/10.1080/14616730802461367

Reagan, A., Michell, L., Kiley, D., Danforth, C., & Dodds, P. (2016). The emotional arcs of stories are dominated by six basic shapes. *EPJ Data Science, 5*(31), 1–12. https://doi.org/10.1140/epjds/s13688-016-0093-1

Reese, E. (2008). Maternal coherence in the Adult Attachment Interview is linked to maternal reminiscing and to children's self concept. *Attachment & Human Development, 10*(4), 451–464. https://doi.org/10.1080/14616730802 461474

Reese, E. (2013). *Tell me a story: Sharing stories to enrich your child's life* (p. 19). New York: Oxford University Press. https://doi.org/10.1093/acprof: osobl/9780199772650.001.0001

Reese, E., & Fivush, R. (1993). Parental styles of talking about the past. *Developmental Psychology, 29*(3), 596. https://doi.org/10.1037/0012-1649 .29.3.596

Reese, E., Fivush, R., Merrill, N., Wang, Q., & McAnally, H. (2017). Adolescents' intergenerational narratives across cultures. *Developmental Psychology, 53*(6), 1142. https://doi.org/10.1037/dev0000309

Reese, E., Haden, C. A., Baker-Ward, L. et al. (2011). Coherence of personal narratives across the lifespan: A multidimensional model and coding method. *Journal of Cognition and Development, 12*(4), 424–462. https://doi.org/10 .1080/15248372.2011.587854

Reese, E., Haden, C., & Fivush, R. (1993). Mother-child conversations about the past: Relationships of style and memory over time. *Cognitive Development, 8*, 403–430. https://doi.org/10.1016/S0885-2014(05)80002-4

Reese, E., Jack, F., & White, N. (2010). Origins of adolescents' autobiographical memories. *Cognitive Development, 25*(4), 352–367. https://doi.org/10 .1016/j.cogdev.2010.08.006

Reese, E., Macfarlane, L., McAnally, H., Robertson, S. J., & Taumoepeau, M. (2020). Coaching in maternal reminiscing with preschoolers leads to elaborative and coherent personal narratives in early adolescence. *Journal of Experimental Child Psychology, 189*, 104707. https://doi.org/10.1016/j .jecp.2019.104707

Reese, E., Meins, E., Fernyhough, C., & Centifanti, L. (2019). Origins of mother–child reminiscing style. *Development and Psychopathology, 31*(2), 631–642. https://doi.org/10.1017/S0954579418000172

Reese, E., & Newcombe, R. (2007). Training mothers in elaborative reminiscing enhances children's autobiographical memory and narrative. *Child Development, 78*(4), 1153–1170. https://doi.org/10.1111/j.1467-8624 .2007.01058.x

Reese, E., Yan, C., Jack, F., & Hayne, H. (2010). Emerging identities: Narrative and self from early childhood to early adolescence. In K. C. McLean & M. Pasupathi (Eds.). *Narrative development in adolescence: Creating the storied self* (pp. 23–43). Boston, MA: Springer. https://doi.org/10.1007/978-0-387-89825-4_2

Ricoeur, P. (1991). Life in quest of narrative. In D. Wood (Ed.). *On Paul Ricoeur: Narrative and interpretation* (pp. 20–33). London: Routledge

Rimé, B. (2009). Emotion elicits the social sharing of emotion: Theory and empirical review. *Emotion review*, *1*(1), 60–85. https://doi.org/10.1177/1754073908097189

Rochat, P. (2018). The ontogeny of human self-consciousness. *Current Directions in Psychological Science*, *27*(5), 345–350. https://doi.org/10.1177/0963721418760236

Rogoff, B., Dahl, A., & Callanan, M. (2018). The importance of understanding children's lived experience. *Developmental Review*, *50*, 5–15. https://doi.org/10.1016/j.dr.2018.05.006

Rosenthal, C. J. (1985). Kinkeeping in the familial division of labor. *Journal of Marriage and the Family*, 965–974. https://doi.org/10.2307/352340

Rubin, D. C. (2021). A conceptual space for episodic and semantic memory. *Memory & Cognition*, 1–14.

Rudek, D. J. (2004). *Reminiscing about past events: Influences on children's deliberate memory and metacognitive skills*. Unpublished doctoral dissertation, Chicago, Illinois: Department of Psychology, Loyola University Chicago.

Salmon, K., & Reese, E. (2016). The benefits of reminiscing with young children. *Current Directions in Psychological Science*, *25*(4), 233–238. https://doi.org/10.1177/0963721416655100

Sameroff, A. (2010). A unified theory of development: A dialectical integration of nature and nurture. *Child Development*, *81*, 6–22. https://doi.org/10.1111/j.1467-8624.2009.01378.x

Schacter, D. L. (2002). *The seven sins of memory: How the mind forgets and remembers*. Boston: Houghton Mifflin Harcourt.

Schacter, D. L., Addis, D. R., & Buckner, R. L. (2007). Remembering the past to imagine the future: The prospective brain. *Nature Reviews Neuroscience*, *8*(9), 657–661. https://doi.org/10.1038/nrn2213

Schectman, M. (2003). Empathic access: The missing ingredient in personal identity. In R. Martin & J. Barresi (Eds.). *Personal identity*, (pp. 238–259). Oxford: Oxford University Press.

Schoppe-Sullivan, S. J., & Fagan, J. (2020). The evolution of fathering research in the 21st century: Persistent challenges, new directions. *Journal of Marriage and Family*, *82*(1), 175–197. https://doi.org/10.1111/jomf.12645

Schröder, L., Keller, H., Kärtner, J. et al. (2013a). Early reminiscing in cultural contexts: Cultural models, maternal reminiscing styles, and children's memories. *Journal of Cognition and Development*, *14*(1), 10–34. https://doi.org/10.1080/15248372.2011.638690

Schröder, L., Keller, H., & Kleis, A. (2013b). Parent-child conversations in three urban middle-class contexts: Mothers and fathers reminisce with their daughters and sons in Costa Rica, Mexico, and Germany. *Actualidades en Psicología, 27*(115), 49–73. https://doi.org/10.15517/ap.v27i115.9885

Schröder, L., Keller, H., Tõugu, P. et al. (2011). Cultural expressions of pre-schoolers' emerging self: Narrative and iconic representations. *Journal of Cognitive Education and Psychology, 10*(1), 77. https://doi.org/10.1891/1945-8959.10.1.77

Squire, L. R. (2004). Memory systems of the brain: A brief history and current perspective. *Neurobiology of Learning and Memory, 82*(3), 171–177. https://doi.org/10.1016/j.nlm.2004.06.005

Stout, D., & Chaminade, T. (2009). Making tools and making sense: Complex, intentional behaviour in human evolution. *Cambridge Archaeological Journal, 19*(1), 85–96. https://doi.org/10.1017/S0959774309000055

Suddendorf, T., Addis, D. R., & Corballis, M. C. (2009). Mental time travel and the shaping of the human mind. *Philosophical Transactions of the Royal Society B: Biological Sciences, 364*(1521), 1317–1324. https://doi.org/10.1098/rstb.2008.0301

Sutton, J. (1998). *Philosophy and memory traces: Descartes to connectionism.* Cambridge: Cambridge University Press.

Sutton, J., & Hodder, I. (2019). Personal memory, the scaffolded mind, and cognitive change in the Neolithic. In I. Hodder (Ed.). *Consciousness, creativity and self at the dawn of settled life* (pp. 209–229). Cambridge: Cambridge University Press. https://doi.org/10.1017/9781108753616

Svane, R. P., Olesen, M. J. R., Kingo, O. S., & Krøjgaard, P. (2021). Gender and parental involvement in parent-child reminiscing in a Scandinavian sample. *Scandinavian Journal of Psychology, 62*(2), 159–169. https://doi.org/10.1111/sjop.12695

Taumoepeau, M., & Reese, E. (2013). Maternal reminiscing, elaborative talk, and children's theory of mind: An intervention study. *First Language, 33*(4), 388–410. https://doi.org/10.1177/0142723713493347

Thorne, A., & McLean, K. C. (2003). Telling traumatic events in adolescence: A study of master narrative positioning. In R. Fivush & C. A. Haden (Eds.). *Autobiographical memory and the construction of a narrative self: Developmental and cultural perspectives* (pp. 169–185). Mahwah: Lawrence Erlbaum Associates.

Thorstad, R., Fivush, R., & Graci, M. (in prep). *Similarity of personal and cultural narratives.* Manuscript in preparation.

Tõugu, P., Tulviste, T., Schröder, L., Keller, H., & De Geer, B. (2012). Content of maternal open-ended questions and statements in reminiscing with their

4-year-olds: Links with independence and interdependence orientation in European contexts. *Memory*, *20*(5), 499–510. https://doi.org/10.1080/09658211.2012.683009

Tulving, E. (1972). Episodic and semantic memory. In E. Tulving & W. Donaldson (Eds.). *Organization of memory* (pp. 382–403). New York: Academic Press.

Tulviste, T., Tõugu, P., Keller, H., Schröder, L., & De Geer, B. (2016). Children's and mothers' contribution to joint reminiscing in different sociocultural contexts: Who speaks and what is said. *Infant and Child Development*, *25*(1), 43–63. https://doi.org/10.1002/icd.1921

Uehara, I. (2015). Developmental changes in memory-related linguistic skills and their relationship to episodic recall in children. *PloS one*, *10*, e0137220. https://doi.org/10.1371/journal.pone.0137220

Verhage, M. L., Schuengel, C., Madigan, S. et al. (2016). Narrowing the transmission gap: A synthesis of three decades of research on intergenerational transmission of attachment. *Psychological Bulletin*, *142*(4), 337–366. https://doi.org/10.1037/bul0000038

Vygotsky, L. S. (1978). *Mind in society: The development of higher psychological processes*. Cambridge, MA: Harvard University Press.

Wang, Q. (2013). The cultured self and remembering. In P. J. Bauer & R. Fivush (Eds.). *The Handbook of Children's Memory Development*. New York: Wiley-Blackwell. https://doi.org/10.1002/9781118597705.ch26

Wang, Q. (2016). Remembering the self in cultural contexts: A cultural dynamic theory of autobiographical memory. *Memory Studies*, *9*(3), 295–304. https://doi.org/10.1177/1750698016645238

Wang, Q. (2021). The cultural foundation of human memory. *Annual Review of Psychology*, *72*, 151–179. https://doi.org/10.1146/annurev-psych-070920-023638

Waters, T. E. A., Bauer, P. J., & Fivush, R. (2014). Autobiographical memory functions of single and recurring events. *Applied Cognitive Psychology*, *28*, 185–195. https://doi.org/10.1002/acp.2976

Waters, T. E., Camia, C., Facompré, C. R., & Fivush, R. (2019). A meta-analytic examination of maternal reminiscing style: Elaboration, gender, and children's cognitive development. *Psychological Bulletin*, *145*(11), 1082. https://doi.org/10.1037/bul0000211

Watson, A.C., Painter, K. M., & Bornstein, M. H. (2001). Longitudinal relations between 2-year-olds' language and 4-year-olds' theory of mind. *Journal of Cognition and Development*, *2*(4), 449–457. https://doi.org/10.1207/s15327647jcd0204_5

Wellman, H. M. (2018). Theory of mind: The state of the art. *European Journal of Developmental Psychology*, *15*, 1–28. https://doi.org/10.1080/17405629.2018.1435413

Wu, Y., & Jobson, L. (2019). Maternal reminiscing and child autobiographical memory elaboration: A meta-analytic review. *Developmental Psychology*, *55*(12), 2505. https://doi.org/10.1037/dev0000821

Zaman, W., & Fivush, R. (2013). Gender differences in elaborative parent–child emotion and play narratives. *Sex Roles*, *68*(9–10), 591–604. https://doi.org/10.1007/s11199-013-0270-7

Cambridge Elements ☰

Child Development

Marc H. Bornstein

Eunice Kennedy Shriver National Institute of Child Health and Human Development, Bethesda

Institute for Fiscal Studies, London

UNICEF, New York City

Marc Bornstein is an Affiliate of the *Eunice Kennedy Shriver* National Institute of Child Health and Human Development, an International Research Fellow at the Institute for Fiscal Studies (London), and UNICEF Senior Advisor for Research for ECD Parenting Programmes. Bornstein is President Emeritus of the Society for Research in Child Development, Editor Emeritus of *Child Development*, and founding Editor of *Parenting: Science and Practice.*

About the Series

Child development is a lively and engaging, yet serious and real-world subject of scientific study that encompasses myriad theories, methods, substantive areas, and applied concerns. Cambridge Elements in Child Development addresses many contemporary topics in child development with unique, comprehensive, and state-of-the-art treatments of principal issues, primary currents of thinking, original perspectives, and empirical contributions to understanding early human development.

Cambridge Elements ≡

Child Development

Printed in the United States
by Baker & Taylor Publisher Services